TO

Ojanny

FROM

Mom & Pop

FAITH

100 Days to Figure Yours Out!

TEEN SERIES deVos

The quoted ideas expressed in this book (but not Scripture verses) are not, in all cases, exact quotations, as some have been edited for clarity and brevity. In all cases, the author has attempted to maintain the speaker's original intent. In some cases, quoted material for this book was obtained from secondary sources, primarily print media. While every effort was made to ensure the accuracy of these sources, the accuracy cannot be guaranteed. For additions, deletions, corrections, or clarifications in future editions of this text, please write Freeman-Smith, LLC.

Scripture quotations are taken from:

The Holy Bible, King James Version

The Holy Bible, New International Version (NIV) Copyright © 1973, 1978, 1984, by International Bible Society. Used by permission of Zondervan Publishing House. All rights reserved.

The New American Standard Bible®, (NASB) Copyright © 1960, 1962, 1963, 1968, 1971, 1972, 1973, 1975, 1977, 1995 by The Lockman Foundation. Used by permission.

The Holy Bible, New King James Version (NKJV) Copyright © 1982 by Thomas Nelson, Inc. Used by permission.

The Holy Bible, New Living Translation, (NLT) Copyright © 1996. Used by permission of Tyndale House Publishers, Inc., Wheaton, Illinois 60189. All rights reserved.

New Century Version®. (NCV) Copyright © 1987, 1988, 1991 by Word Publishing, a division of Thomas Nelson, Inc. All rights reserved. Used by permission.

The Message (MSG) This edition issued by contractual arrangement with NavPress, a division of The Navigators, U.S.A. Originally published by NavPress in English as THE MESSAGE: The Bible in Contemporary Language copyright 2002-2003 by Eugene Peterson. All rights reserved.

The Holman Christian Standard Bible™ (HOLMAN CSB) Copyright © 1999, 2000, 2001 by Holman Bible Publishers. Used by permission.

Cover Design by Kim Russell / Wahoo Designs
Page Layout by Bart Dawson

ISBN 978-1-60587-098-4

Printed in the United States of America

FAITH

100 Days to Figure Yours Out!

Introduction

Figuring out your faith can be tough sometimes, but never impossible. This book contains 100 brief devotional readings that are intended to help you strengthen your faith—and figure it out—by focusing on God's truths. And make no mistake: God's truths are both eternal and unchanging.

Every life—including yours—is a series of wins and losses, celebrations and disappointments, joys and sorrows. Every step of the way, through every triumph and tragedy, God will stand by your side and strengthen you . . . if you have faith in Him.

Would you like to build a stronger faith and better future? If so, ask for God's help many times each day . . . starting with a regular, heartfelt morning devotional. When you do, you will change your day . . . and your life.

To Figure Out Your Faith, You Need to Put God First

You shall have no other gods before Me.

Exodus 20:3 NKJV

To figure out your faith, you'll need to start by putting God in His rightful place: first place. So here's the million dollar question: Who's in charge of your heart? Is it God, or is it something else? Have you given Christ your heart, your soul, your talents, your time, and your testimony? Or are you giving Him little more than a few hours each Sunday morning?

In the book of Exodus, God warns that we should place no gods before Him. Yet all too often, we place our Lord in second, third, or fourth place as we worship other things. When we unwittingly place possessions or relationships above our love for the Creator, we create big problems for ourselves.

Have you chosen to allow God to rule your heart? Make certain that the honest answer to this question is a resounding yes. In the life of every thoughtful believer, God comes first. And that's precisely the place that He deserves in your heart.

One with God is a majority.

Billy Graham

God is the beyond in the midst of our life.

Dietrich Bonhoeffer

You can't get second things by putting them first;
you can get second things only
by putting first things first.

C. S. Lewis

We become whatever we are committed to.

Rick Warren

Figuring Out Your Faith: Write down a few of your own ideas about putting God first.

I will always put god first in my life no matter what happens I will put god first.

To Figure Out Your Faith, You Need to Understand That God Is Love

*God is love, and the one who remains in love remains in God,
and God remains in him.*

I John 4:16 Holman CSB

God is love. It's a sweeping statement, a profoundly important description of what God is and how God works. God's love is perfect. When we open our hearts to His perfect love, we are touched by the Creator's hand, and we are transformed.

Today, even if you can only carve out a few quiet moments, offer sincere prayers of thanksgiving to your Father. Thank Him for His blessings and His love. As you sit in silence, open your heart to the Father, and do your best to sense His presence. When you do, you'll discover the genuine peace that only the Creator can provide. That peace, of course, flows from the loving heart of God. You can experience His peace and His love today . . . and you should.

The life of faith is a daily exploration
of the constant and countless ways in which
God's grace and love are experienced.

Eugene Peterson

If you have an obedience problem,
you have a love problem.
Focus your attention on God's love.

Henry Blackaby

I can tell you, from personal experience
of walking with God for over fifty years,
that He is the Lover of my soul.

Vonette Bright

Figuring Out Your Faith: Write down a few of your
own ideas about God's love.

I ♡ god. And
I ♡ his ♡.

When You Have Questions, Take Them to God

*Now if any of you lacks wisdom, he should ask God,
who gives to all generously and without criticizing,
and it will be given to him. But let him ask in faith without
doubting. For the doubter is like the surging sea,
driven and tossed by the wind.*

James 1:5-6 Holman CSB

Figuring out your faith means answering lots of questions. But sometimes, there are so many questions and so few answers! If you find yourself with more Q than A, don't panic. Even the most faithful Christians are overcome by occasional bouts of fear and doubt. You are no different.

When you feel that your faith is being tested to its limits, seek the comfort and assurance of the One who sent His Son as a sacrifice for you. And remember: Even when you feel very distant from God, God is never distant from you. When you sincerely seek His presence, He will touch your heart, calm your fears, and restore your soul.

When there is perplexity there is always guidance—
not always at the moment we ask, but in good time,
which is God's time. There is no need to fret and stew.

Elisabeth Elliot

We are finding we don't have such a gnawing need to
know the answers when we know the Answer.

Gloria Gaither

Be to the world a sign that while we as Christians
do not have all the answers,
we do know and care about the questions.

Billy Graham

Figuring Out Your Faith: Write down a few of your
own ideas about questions that bug you.

?

_____

_____

_____

_____

_____

When Your Faith Is Tested, Remember That God Can Handle Any Problem

Give your burdens to the Lord, and he will take care of you.
He will not permit the godly to slip and fall.

Psalm 55:22 NLT

When your faith is tested, you can be sure of this: God is far bigger than your problems. So whatever "it" is, remember that God can handle it.

Life isn't always easy. Far from it! Sometimes, life can be very, very tough. But even then, even during our darkest moments, we're protected by a loving Heavenly Father. When we're worried, God can reassure us; when we're sad, God can comfort us. When our hearts are broken, God is not just near, He is here. So we must lift our thoughts and prayers to Him. When we do, He will answer our prayers. Why? Because He is our shepherd, and He has promised to protect us now and forever.

You may not know what you are ...
you only know that God knows what ...

Oswald Chambers

The next time you're disappointed, don't panic.
Don't give up. Just be patient and let God
remind you he's still in control.

Max Lucado

Jesus does not say, "There is no storm."
He says, "I am here, do not toss, but trust."

Vance Havner

Figuring Out Your Faith: Write down a few of your
own ideas about tough times.

Don't worry
about anything
be patient like what
god said in the bible.

To Figure Out Your Faith, Keep Studying God's Word

For I am not ashamed of the gospel, because it is God's power for salvation to everyone who believes.

Romans 1:16 Holman CSB

The Bible can be a powerful tool for strengthening your faith. George Mueller observed, "The vigor of our spiritual lives will be in exact proportion to the place held by the Bible in our lives and in our thoughts."

As a Christian, you are called upon to study God's Holy Word and then apply it to your life. When you do, you will be blessed.

The Bible is a priceless gift, a tool for Christians to use as they share the Good News of their Savior, Christ Jesus. Too many Christians, however, keep their spiritual tool kits tightly closed and out of sight. Jonathan Edwards advised, "Be assiduous in reading the Holy Scriptures. This is the fountain whence all knowledge in divinity must be derived. Therefore let not this treasure lie by you neglected." God's Holy Word is, indeed, a priceless, one-of-a-kind treasure. Handle it with care, but, more importantly, handle it every day.

The instrument of our sanctification is the Word of God.
The Spirit of God brings to our minds the precepts and
doctrines of truth, and applies them with power.
The truth is our sanctifier. If we do not hear or read it,
we will not grow in sanctification.

C. H. Spurgeon

God gives us a compass and a Book of promises and
principles—the Bible—and lets us make our decisions day
by day as we sense the leading of His Spirit.
This is how we grow.

Warren Wiersbe

Figuring Out Your Faith: Write down a few of your
own ideas about Bible study.

Sometimes I read
gods word.

Your Faith Should Be Contagious

*Whatever you do, do it enthusiastically,
as something done for the Lord and not for men.*

Colossians 3:23 Holman CSB

The stronger your faith, the better you can rise above the inevitable stresses of everyday life. And the more enthused you are about your faith, the better you can share it.

Are you genuinely excited about your faith? And do you make your enthusiasm known to those around you? Or are you a "silent ambassador" for Christ? God's preference is clear: He intends that you stand before others and proclaim your faith.

Genuine, heartfelt Christianity is contagious. If you enjoy a life-altering relationship with God, that relationship will have an impact on others—perhaps a profound impact.

Does Christ reign over your life? Then share your testimony and your excitement. The world needs both.

We act as though comfort and luxury were
the chief requirements of life, when all we need
to make us really happy is something
to be enthusiastic about.

Charles Kingsley

Your enthusiasm will be infectious, stimulating,
and attractive to others. They will love you for it.
They will go for you and with you.

Norman Vincent Peale

Don't take hold of a thing unless you want
that thing to take hold of you.

E. Stanley Jones

Figuring Out Your Faith: Write down a few of your
own ideas about the power of enthusiasm.

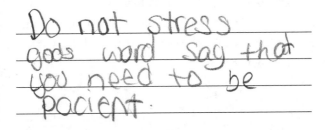

Do not stress
gods word say that
you need to be
pacient.

To Build Your Faith, Trust God's Promises

God—His way is perfect; the word of the Lord is pure.
He is a shield to all who take refuge in Him.

Psalm 18:30 Holman CSB

God has made quite a few promises to you, and He intends to keep every single one of them. You will find these promises in a book like no other: the Holy Bible. The Bible is your roadmap for life here on earth and for life eternal—as a believer, you are called upon to trust its promises, to follow its commandments, and to share its Good News.

God has made promises to all of humanity and to you. God's promises never fail and they never grow old. You must trust those promises and share them with your family, with your friends, and with the world . . . starting now . . . and ending never.

God's promises are medicine for the broken heart.
Let Him comfort you. And, after He has comforted you,
try to share that comfort with somebody else.
It will do both of you good.

Warren Wiersbe

The stars may fall, but God's promises
will stand and be fulfilled.

J. I. Packer

There are four words I wish we would never forget,
and they are, "God keeps His word."

Charles Swindoll

Figuring Out Your Faith: Write down a few of your
own ideas about God's promises.

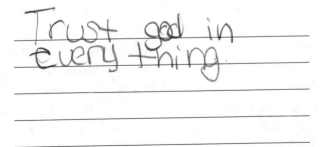

Trust god in
every thing.

To Build Your Faith,
Entrust Your Hopes to God

You, Lord, give true peace to those who depend on you,
because they trust you.

Isaiah 26:3 NCV

There are few sadder sights on earth than the sight of a girl or guy who has lost hope. In difficult times, hope can be elusive, but those who place their faith in God's promises need never lose it. After all, God is good; His love endures; He has promised His children the gift of eternal life. And, God keeps His promises.

If you find yourself falling into the spiritual traps of worry and discouragement, seek the healing touch of Jesus and the encouraging words of fellow believers. And if you find a friend in need, remind him or her of the peace that is found through a genuine relationship with Christ. It was Christ who promised, "I have told you these things so that in Me you may have peace. In the world you have suffering. But take courage! I have conquered the world." (John 16:33 Holman CSB). This world can be a place of trials and troubles, but as believers, we are secure. God has promised us peace, joy, and eternal life. And, of course, God keeps His promises today, tomorrow, and forever.

Hope is faith holding out its hand in the dark.
Barbara Johnson

The will of God is the most delicious
and delightful thing in the universe.
Hannah Whitall Smith

It is more serious to lose hope than to sin.
John of Carpathos

Figuring Out Your Faith: Write down a few of your own ideas about entrusting your hopes to God.

I love god I will never be in a worry because I know that god is whith me.

It's Always the Right Time to Start Celebrating Your Life and Your Faith

This is the day the Lord has made;
let us rejoice and be glad in it.

Psalm 118:24 Holman CSB

Do you want to know God more intimately? Try this: celebrate the life He has given you.

Do you feel like celebrating today? If you're a believer, you should. When you allow Christ to reign over your heart, today and every day should be a time for joyful celebration.

What do you expect from the day ahead? Are you expecting God to do wonderful things, or are you living beneath a cloud of worry and doubt? The words of Psalm 118:24 remind us that every day is a gift from God. So whatever this day holds for you, begin it and end it with God as your partner and Christ as your Savior. And throughout the day, give thanks to the One who created you and saved you. God's love for you is infinite. Accept it; celebrate it; and be thankful.

Joy is the great note all throughout the Bible.
Oswald Chambers

Some of us seem so anxious about avoiding hell
that we forget to celebrate our journey toward heaven.
Philip Yancey

If you can forgive the person you were, accept the person
you are, and believe in the person you will become,
you are headed for joy. So celebrate your life.
Barbara Johnson

Unparalleled joy and victory come from allowing
Christ to do "the hard thing" with us.
Beth Moore

Figuring Out Your Faith: Write down a few of your
own ideas about celebrating life.

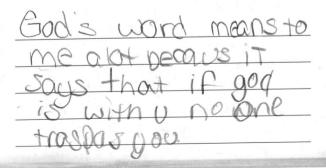

God's word means to
me a lot becaus it
says that if god
is with u no one
traspas you

Faith in Christ
Equals Eternal Life

*For God so loved the world that he gave his
one and only Son, that whoever believes in him shall not
perish but have eternal life.*

John 3:16 NIV

Your decision to allow Christ to reign over your heart is the pivotal decision of your life. It is a decision that you cannot ignore. It is a decision that is yours and yours alone.

God's love for you is deeper and more profound than you can imagine. God's love for you is so great that He sent His only Son to this earth to die for your sins and to offer you the priceless gift of eternal life. Now, you must decide whether or not to accept God's gift. Will you ignore it or embrace it? Will you return it or neglect it? Will you accept Christ's love and build a lifelong relationship with Him, or will you turn away from Him and take a different path?

Accept God's gift now: allow His Son to preside over your heart, your thoughts, and your life, starting this very instant.

It's your heart that Jesus longs for: your will to be made
His own with self on the cross forever,
and Jesus alone on the throne.

Ruth Bell Graham

The amount of power you experience to live a victorious,
triumphant Christian life is directly proportional to the
freedom you give the Spirit to be Lord of your life!

Anne Graham Lotz

Choose Jesus Christ! Deny yourself, take up the Cross,
and follow Him—for the world must be shown.
The world must see, in us, a discernible,
visible, startling difference.

Elisabeth Elliot

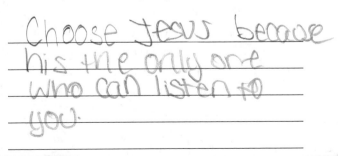

Figuring Out Your Faith: Write down a few of your
own ideas about accepting Christ.

Choose Jesus because
his the only one
who can listen to
you.

Remember That Character Counts

In all things showing yourself to be a pattern of good works; in doctrine showing integrity, reverence, incorruptibility . . . .
Titus 2:7 NKJV

Beth Moore correctly observed, "Those who walk in truth walk in liberty." Godly guys and girls agree. As believers in Christ, we must seek to live each day with discipline, honesty, and faith. When we do, at least two things happen: integrity becomes a habit, and God blesses us because of our obedience to Him. Living a life of integrity isn't always the easiest way, but in the long run, it's the more peaceful—and less stressful—way to live.

Character isn't built overnight; it is built slowly over a lifetime. It is the sum of every sensible choice, every honorable decision, and every honest word. It is forged on the anvil of sincerity and polished by the virtue of fairness. Character is a precious thing—preserve yours at all costs.

Integrity is the glue that holds our way of life together. We must constantly strive to keep our integrity intact. When wealth is lost, nothing is lost; when health is lost, something is lost; when character is lost, all is lost.

Billy Graham

The man who cannot believe in himself cannot believe in anything else. The basis of all integrity and character is whatever faith we have in our own integrity.

Roy L. Smith

Image is what people think we are; integrity is what we really are.

John Maxwell

Figuring Out Your Faith: Write down a few of your own ideas about ways you can strengthen your character.

I think we are really suppose to care about our character

Remember That You Are Richly Blessed

The Lord bless you and keep you; the Lord make His face shine upon you, and be gracious to you.

Numbers 6:24-25 NKJV

Have you counted your blessings lately? If you sincerely wish to follow in Christ's footsteps, you should make thanksgiving a habit, a regular part of your daily routine.

How has God blessed you? First and foremost, He has given you the gift of eternal life through the sacrifice of His only begotten Son, but the blessings don't stop there. Today, take time to make a partial list of God's gifts to you: the talents, the opportunities, the possessions, and the relationships that you may, on occasion, take for granted. And then, when you've spent sufficient time listing your blessings, offer a prayer of gratitude to the Giver of all things good . . . and, to the best of your ability, use your gifts for the glory of His kingdom.

It is when we give ourselves to be a blessing that
we can especially count on the blessing of God.

Andrew Murray

We prevent God from giving us the great spiritual gifts
He has in store for us,
because we do not give thanks for daily gifts.

Dietrich Bonhoeffer

Nobody ever outgrows Scripture;
the book widens and deepens with our years.

C. H. Spurgeon

Get rich quick! Count your blessings!

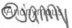
Anonymous

Figuring Out Your Faith: Write down a few of your
own ideas about your blessings.

Give your life to
good and give thanks
to him every day

To Live the Life God Wants You to Live, You Must Make Wise Choices

*But the wisdom from above is first pure, then peace-loving,
gentle, compliant, full of mercy and good fruits,
without favoritism and hypocrisy.*

James 3:17 Holman CSB

Your life is a series of choices. From the instant you
wake up in the morning until the moment you
nod off to sleep at night, you make countless decisions—decisions about the things you do, decisions about
the words you speak, and decisions about the way that you
choose to direct your thoughts.

As a believer who has been transformed by the love
of Jesus, you have every reason to make wise choices. But
sometimes, when the stresses of the daily grind threaten to
grind you up and spit you out, you may make choices that
are displeasing to God. When you do, you'll pay a price because you'll forfeit the happiness and the peace that might
otherwise have been yours.

...use to consider the kind of Christian you
...d of Christian you want to become—ask
...ou're sitting on the fence or standing in
...ice is yours . . . and so are the conse-

The greatest choice any man makes is
to let God choose for him.

Vance Havner

Every step of your life's journey is a choice . . .
and the quality of those choices determines
the quality of the journey.

Criswell Freeman

Figuring Out Your Faith: Write down a few of your
own ideas about the value of making wise choices.

_____

_____

_____

_____

_____

Remember That God Wants You to Be a Courageous Christian

Be strong and courageous, and do the work. Don't be afraid or discouraged, for the Lord God, my God, is with you. He won't leave you or forsake you.

I Chronicles 28:20 Holman CSB

Because we are saved by your faith in the risen Christ, we can have hope for the future, no matter how desperate our circumstances may seem. After all, God has promised that we are His throughout eternity. And, He has told us that we must place our hopes in Him.

Today, summon the courage to follow God. Even if your faith is tested, even if the path seems difficult, even if your heart is fearful, trust your Heavenly Father and follow Him. Trust Him with your day and your life. Do His work, care for His children, and share His Good News. Let Him guide your steps. He will not lead you astray.

Down through the centuries, in times of trouble and trial, God has brought courage to the hearts of those who love Him. The Bible is filled with assurances of God's help and comfort in every kind of trouble which might cause fears to arise in the human heart.

You can look ahead with promise, hope, and joy.

Billy Graham

Be careful how you live. You may be the only Bible some person ever reads.

William J. Toms

The central Christian belief is that Christ's death has somehow put us right with God and given us a fresh start.

C. S. Lewis

Figuring Out Your Faith: Write down a few of your own ideas about what it means to be a courageous Christian.

_____

_____

_____

_____

Focus on Faith, Not Appearances

As the water reflects the face, so the heart reflects the person.
Proverbs 27:19 Holman CSB

The world sees you as you appear to be; God sees you as you really are. He sees your heart, and He understands your intentions. The opinions of others should be relatively unimportant to you; however, God's view of you—His understanding of your actions, your thoughts, and your motivations—should be vitally important.

Few things in life are more futile than "keeping up appearances" in order to impress your friends and your dates—yet the media would have you believe otherwise. The media would have you believe that everything depends on the color of your hair, the condition of your wardrobe, and the model of the car you drive. But nothing could be further from the truth. What is important, of course, is pleasing your Father in heaven. You please Him when your intentions are pure and your actions are just. When you do, you will be blessed today, tomorrow, and forever.

Too many Christians have geared their program to please,
to entertain, and to gain favor from this world.
We are concerned with how much, instead of how little,
like this age we can become.

Billy Graham

Outside appearances, things like the clothes you wear or
the car you drive, are important to other people
but totally unimportant to God. Trust God.

Marie T. Freeman

Fashion is an enduring testimony to the fact that
we live quite consciously before the eyes of others.

John Eldredge

Figuring Out Your Faith: Write down a few of your
own ideas about looking good versus being good.

_____

_____

_____

_____

_____

Remember That
It Pays to Be Disciplined

But I discipline my body and bring it into subjection,
lest, when I have preached to others,
I myself should become disqualified.

I Corinthians 9:27 NKJV

Face it: God doesn't reward laziness, misbehavior, or apathy. To the contrary, He expects His followers to behave with dignity and discipline. But sometimes, it's extremely difficult to be dignified and disciplined. Why? Because the world wants us to believe that dignified, self-disciplined behavior is going out of style.

Face facts: Life's greatest rewards aren't likely to fall into your lap. To the contrary, your greatest accomplishments will probably require lots of work, which is perfectly fine with God. After all, He knows that you're up to the task, and He has big plans for you. God will do His part to fulfill those plans, and the rest, of course, is up to you.

Now, are you steadfast in your determination to be a self-disciplined person? If so, congratulations . . . if not, reread this little essay—and keep reading it—until God's message finally sinks in.

The alternative to discipline is disaster.

Vance Havner

Personal humility is a spiritual discipline
and the hallmark of the service of Jesus.

Franklin Graham

Discipline is training that develops and corrects.

Charles Stanley

As we seek to become disciples of Jesus Christ, we should
never forget that the word disciple is directly related to
the word discipline. To be a disciple of the Lord Jesus
Christ is to know His discipline.

Dennis Swanberg

Figuring Out Your Faith: Write down a few of your
own ideas about the value of discipline.

_____

_____

_____

_____

_____

To Strengthen Your Faith, You Should Follow Jesus Every Day

"Follow Me," Jesus told them, "and I will make you into fishers of men!" Immediately they left their nets and followed Him.

Mark 1:17-18 Holman CSB

Can you honestly say that you're passionate about your faith and that you're really following Jesus? Hopefully so. But if you're preoccupied with other things—or if you're strictly a one-day-a-week Christian—then you're in need of a major-league spiritual makeover.

Jesus doesn't want you to be a lukewarm believer; Jesus wants you to be a "new creation" through Him. And that's exactly what you should want for yourself, too. Nothing is more important than your wholehearted commitment to your Creator and to His only begotten Son. Your faith must never be an afterthought; it must be your ultimate priority, your ultimate possession, and your ultimate passion.

You are the recipient of Christ's love. Accept it enthusiastically and share it passionately. Jesus deserves your undivided attention. And when you give it to Him, you'll be forever grateful that you did.

Imagine the spiritual strength the disciples drew from walking hundreds of miles with Jesus . . . 3 John 4.

John Maxwell

Jesus challenges you and me to keep our focus daily on the cross of His will if we want to be His disciples.

Anne Graham Lotz

It's your heart that Jesus longs for:
your will to be made His own with self on the cross forever, and Jesus alone on the throne.

Ruth Bell Graham

Figuring Out Your Faith: Write down a few of your own ideas about following Christ.

_____

_____

_____

_____

_____

Remember That Every Day Is a New Beginning

*You are being renewed in the spirit of your minds;
you put on the new man, the one created according to
God's likeness in righteousness and purity of the truth.*

Ephesians 4:23-24 Holman CSB

Each new day offers countless opportunities to serve God, to seek His will, and to obey His teachings. But each day also offers countless opportunities to stray from God's commandments and to wander far from His path.

Sometimes, we wander aimlessly in a wilderness of our own making, but God has better plans of us. And, whenever we ask Him to renew our strength and guide our steps, He does so.

Consider this day a new beginning. Consider it a fresh start, a renewed opportunity to serve your Creator with willing hands and a loving heart. Ask God to renew your sense of purpose as He guides your steps. Today is a glorious opportunity to serve God. Seize that opportunity while you can; tomorrow may indeed be too late.

No matter how badly we have failed,
we can always get up and begin again.
Our God is the God of new beginnings.

Warren Wiersbe

Sometimes your medicine bottle has on it,
"Shake well before using." That is what God has to do
with some of His people. He has to shake them well
before they are ever usable.

Vance Havner

No man need stay the way he is.

Harry Emerson Fosdick

Figuring Out Your Faith: Write down a few of your
own ideas about making a new beginning.

_____

_____

_____

_____

_____

Genuine Faith Means Standing Up for Your Beliefs

I know whom I have believed and am persuaded that He is able to guard what has been entrusted to me until that day.

2 Timothy 1:12 Holman CSB

In describing one's beliefs, actions are far better descriptors than words. Yet far too many of us spend more energy talking about our beliefs than living by them—with predictable consequences.

Is your life a picture book of your creed? Are your actions congruent with your beliefs? Are you willing to practice the philosophy that you preach? If so, you'll most certainly feel better about yourself.

Today and every day, make certain that your actions are guided by God's Word and by the conscience that He has placed in your heart. Don't treat your faith as if it were separate from your everyday life. Weave your beliefs into the very fabric of your day. When you do, God will honor your good works, and your good works will honor God.

I do not seek to understand that I may believe,
but I believe in order to understand.

St. Augustine

Belief is not the result of an intellectual act;
it is the result of an act of my will whereby
I deliberately commit myself.

Oswald Chambers

You may as well quit reading and hearing
the Word of God and give it to the devil if you do not
desire to live according to it.

Martin Luther

Figuring Out Your Faith: Write down a few of your
own ideas about standing up for your beliefs.

_____

_____

_____

_____

_____

Remember That There's Always Room for Spiritual Growth

So let us stop going over the basics of Christianity again and again. Let us go on instead and become mature in our understanding.

Hebrews 6:1 NLT

A re you about as mature as you're ever going to be? Hopefully not! When it comes to your faith, God doesn't intend for you to become "fully grown," at least not in this lifetime.

As a Christian, you should continue to grow in the love and the knowledge of your Savior as long as you live. How? By studying God's Word, by obeying His commandments, and by allowing His Son to reign over your heart.

Are you continually seeking to become a more mature believer? Hopefully so, because that's exactly what you owe to God and to yourself.

A person who gazes and keeps on gazing at Jesus
becomes like him in appearance.

E. Stanley Jones

The Scriptures were not given for our information,
but for our transformation.

D. L. Moody

Approach the Scriptures not so much as a manual of
Christian principles but as the testimony of God's friends
on what it means to walk with him through
a thousand different episodes.

John Eldredge

Figuring Out Your Faith: Write down a few of your
own ideas about spiritual growth.

_____

_____

_____

_____

_____

Remember That Nothing Can Separate You from Christ's Love

For I am persuaded that neither death nor life,
nor angels nor rulers, nor things present, nor things to come,
nor powers, nor height, nor depth, nor any other created thing
will have the power to separate us from the love of God
that is in Christ Jesus our Lord!

Romans 8:38-39 Holman CSB

How much does Christ love us? More than we, as mere human beings, can comprehend. His love is perfect and steadfast. Even though we are imperfect and wayward, the Good Shepherd cares for us still. Even though we have fallen far short of the Father's commandments, Christ loves us with a power and depth that are beyond our understanding. The sacrifice that Jesus made upon the cross was made for each of us, and His love endures to the edge of eternity and beyond.

Christ's love changes everything, including your relationships. When you accept His gift of grace, you are transformed, not only for today, but also for all eternity.

Jesus is waiting patiently for you to invite Him into your heart. Please don't make Him wait a single minute longer.

God is my Heavenly Father.
He loves me with an everlasting love.
The proof of that is the Cross.

Elisabeth Elliot

Live your lives in love, the same sort of love which Christ gives us, and which He perfectly expressed when He gave Himself as a sacrifice to God.

Corrie ten Boom

Figuring Out Your Faith: Write down a few of your own ideas about Christ's love.

_____

_____

_____

_____

_____

If You Want to Strengthen Your Faith, Get Involved in a Church

*And I also say to you that you are Peter, and on this rock
I will build My church, and the forces of Hades will not
overpower it. I will give you the keys of the kingdom of
heaven, and whatever you bind on earth will have been
bound in heaven, and whatever you loose on earth
will have been loosed in heaven.*

Matthew 16:18-19 Holman CSB

A good way to figure out the kind of person you want to become is by worshiping with people who love and respect you. That's one reason (but certainly not the only reason) that you should be an active member of a supportive congregation.

Every believer—including you—needs to be part of a community of faith. Your association with fellow Christians should be uplifting, enlightening, encouraging, and consistent.

Are you an active member of your fellowship? Are you a builder of bridges inside the four walls of your church and outside it? Do you contribute your time and your talents to a close-knit band of hope-filled believers? Hopefully so.

The fellowship of believers is intended to be a powerful tool for spreading God's Good News and uplifting His children. God intends for you to be a fully contributing member of that fellowship. Your intentions should be the same.

Only participation in the full life of a local church builds spiritual muscle.

Rick Warren

In God's economy you will be hard-pressed to find many examples of successful "Lone Rangers."

Luci Swindoll

Figuring Out Your Faith: Write down a few of your own ideas about the importance of getting involved in a church.

_____

_____

_____

_____

To Live the Life God Wants You to Live, Listen to Your Conscience

*Now the goal of our instruction is love from a pure heart,
a good conscience, and a sincere faith.*

I Timothy 1:5 Holman CSB

Billy Graham correctly observed, "Most of us follow our conscience as we follow a wheelbarrow. We push it in front of us in the direction we want to go." To do so, of course, is a profound mistake. Yet all of us, on occasion, have failed to listen to the voice that God planted in our hearts, and all of us have suffered the consequences.

God gave you a conscience for a very good reason: to make your path conform to His will. Wise believers make it a practice to listen carefully to that quiet internal voice. Count yourself among that number. When your conscience speaks, listen and learn. In all likelihood, God is trying to get His message through. And in all likelihood, it is a message that you desperately need to hear.

To go against one's conscience is neither safe nor right.
Here I stand. I cannot do otherwise.

Martin Luther

The convicting work of the Holy Spirit awakens,
disturbs, and judges.

Franklin Graham

A good conscience is a continual feast.

Francis Bacon

God desires that we become spiritually healthy enough
through faith to have a conscience that rightly interprets
the work of the Holy Spirit.

Beth Moore

Figuring Out Your Faith: Write down a few of your
own ideas about the value of listening to your
conscience.

_____

_____

_____

_____

If You Want to Find Fulfillment, You Must Look for It in the Right Places

I am the Gate. Anyone who goes through me will be cared for—will freely go in and out, and find pasture.
A thief is only there to steal and kill and destroy.
I came so they can have real and eternal life, more and better life than they ever dreamed of. I am the Good Shepherd.
The Good Shepherd puts the sheep before himself, sacrifices himself if necessary.

John 10:9-11 MSG

Where can we find fulfillment and contentment? Is it a result of wealth, or power, or beauty, or fame? Hardly. Genuine contentment is a gift from God to those who trust Him and follow His commandments.

Our modern world seems preoccupied with the search for happiness. We are bombarded with messages telling us that happiness depends upon the acquisition of material possessions. These messages are false. Enduring peace is not the result of our acquisitions; it is a spiritual gift from God to those who obey Him and accept His will.

If we don't find contentment in God, we will never find it anywhere else. But, if we seek Him and obey Him, we will be blessed with an inner peace that is beyond human understanding. When God dwells at the center of our lives, peace and contentment will belong to us just as surely as we belong to God.

God is most glorified in us when we
are most satisfied in Him.

John Piper

By trying to grab fulfillment everywhere,
we find it nowhere.

Elisabeth Elliot

Figuring Out Your Faith: Write down a few of your own ideas about what contentment means to you.

_____

_____

_____

_____

_____

Remember That
Your Attitude Matters

Set your minds on what is above,
not on what is on the earth.

Colossians 3:2 Holman CSB

The Christian life is a cause for celebration, but sometimes we don't feel much like celebrating. In fact, when the weight of the world seems to bear down upon our shoulders, celebration may be the last thing on our minds . . . but it shouldn't be. As God's children we are all blessed beyond measure on good days and bad. This day is a non-renewable resource: once it's gone, it's gone forever. We should give thanks for this day while using it for the glory of God.

So today, and every day hereafter, celebrate the life that God has given you. Think optimistically about yourself and your future. Give thanks to the One who has given you everything, and trust in your heart that He wants to give you so much more.

The mind is like a clock that is constantly running down.
It has to be wound up daily with good thoughts.

Fulton J. Sheen

The things we think are the things that feed our souls.
If we think on pure and lovely things,
we shall grow pure and lovely like them;
and the converse is equally true.

Hannah Whitall Smith

I may not be able to change the world I see around me,
but I can change the way I see the world within me.

John Maxwell

Figuring Out Your Faith: Write down a few of your own ideas about how your attitude impacts your faith.

_____

_____

_____

_____

You Faith Will Be Tested Because Evil Exists, and It's Dangerous

Take your stand with God's loyal community and live,
or chase after phantoms of evil and die.

Proverbs 11:19 MSG

The better you get to know God, the more you'll understand how God wants you to respond to evil. And make no mistake, this world is inhabited by quite a few people who are very determined to do evil things. The devil and his human helpers are working 24/7 to cause pain and heartbreak in every corner of the globe . . . including your corner. So you'd better beware.

Your job, if you choose to accept it, is to recognize evil and fight it. The moment that you decide to fight evil whenever you see it, you can no longer be a lukewarm, half-hearted Christian. And, when you are no longer a lukewarm Christian, God rejoices while the devil despairs.

When will you choose to get serious about fighting the evils of our world? Before you answer that question, consider this: in the battle of good versus evil, the devil never takes a day off . . . and neither should you.

Rebuke the Enemy in your own name and he laughs;
command him in the name of Christ and he flees.

John Eldredge

He who passively accepts evil is as much involved in it as
he who helps to perpetrate it. He who accepts evil without
protesting against it is really cooperating with it.

Martin Luther King, Jr.

God loves you, and He yearns for you to turn away from
the path of evil. You need His forgiveness,
and you need Him to come into your life
and remake you from within.

Billy Graham

Figuring Out Your Faith: Write down a few of your
own ideas about evil.

_____

_____

_____

_____

_____

To Figure Out Your Faith, You Should Spend Time with God Every Morning

Morning by morning he wakens me and opens my understanding to his will. The Sovereign Lord has spoken to me, and I have listened.

Isaiah 50:4-5 NLT

Want to figure out your faith? Then schedule a meeting with God every day.

Daily life is a tapestry of habits, and no habit is more important to your spiritual health than the discipline of daily prayer and devotion to the Creator. When you begin each day with your head bowed and your heart lifted, you are reminded of God's love and God's laws.

When you do engage in a regular regime of worship and praise, God will reward you for your wisdom and your obedience. Each new day is a gift from God, and if you're wise, you'll spend a few quiet moments thanking the Giver. It's a wonderful way to start your day.

A person with no devotional life generally struggles
with faith and obedience.

Charles Stanley

Mark it down. God never turns away the honest seeker.
Go to God with your questions.
You may not find all the answers, but in finding God,
you know the One who does.

Max Lucado

Maintenance of the devotional mood is indispensable to
success in the Christian life.

A. W. Tozer

Figuring Out Your Faith: Write down a few of your
own ideas about the value of a daily devotional.

_____

_____

_____

_____

_____

To Strengthen Your Faith, It Pays to Date People Who Honor God

We must obey God rather than men.

Acts 5:29 Holman CSB

Is God a part of your dating life? Hopefully so. If you sincerely want to know God, then you should date people who feel the same way.

If you're still searching for Mr. or Mrs. Right (while trying to avoid falling in love with Mr. or Mrs. Wrong), be patient, be prudent, and be picky. Look for someone whose values you respect, whose behavior you approve of, and whose faith you admire. Remember that appearances can be deceiving and tempting, so watch your step. And when it comes to the important task of building a lifetime relationship with the guy or girl of your dreams, pray about it!

When it comes to your dating life, God wants to give His approval—or not—but He won't give it until He's asked. So ask, listen, and decide accordingly.

We discover our role in life through
our relationships with others.

Rick Warren

Make God's will the focus of your life day by day.
If you seek to please Him and Him alone,
you'll find yourself satisfied with life.

Kay Arthur

Line by line, moment by moment, special times
are etched into our memories in the permanent ink of
everlasting love in our relationships.

Gloria Gaither

Figuring Out Your Faith: Write down a few of your
own ideas about what it means to date wisely.

_____

_____

_____

_____

_____

To Strengthen Your Faith, Praise God Early and Often

I will praise You with my whole heart.

Psalm 138:1 NKJV

If you're like most folks on the planet, you're busy. Your life is probably hectic, demanding, and complicated. And when the demands of life leave you rushing from place to place with scarcely a moment to spare, you may not take time to praise your Creator. Big mistake.

The Bible makes it clear: it pays to praise God. Worship and praise should be a part of everything you do. Otherwise, you quickly lose perspective as you fall prey to the demands of everyday life.

Do you sincerely desire to know God in a more meaningful way? Then praise Him for who He is and for what He has done for you. And please don't wait until Sunday morning—praise Him all day long, every day, for as long as you live . . . and then for all eternity.

Two wings are necessary to lift our souls toward God: prayer and praise. Prayer asks. Praise accepts the answer.

Mrs. Charles E. Cowman

Praise opens the window of our hearts, preparing us to walk more closely with God. Prayer raises the window of our spirit, enabling us to listen more clearly to the Father.

Max Lucado

Most of the verses written about praise in God's Word were voiced by people faced with crushing heartaches, injustice, treachery, slander, and scores of other difficult situations.

Joni Eareckson Tada

Figuring Out Your Faith: Write down a few of your own ideas about praising God.

_____

_____

_____

_____

_____

When Your Faith Is Tested, God Is Always Ready to Help

God is our refuge and strength,
a helper who is always found in times of trouble.
Psalm 46:1 Holman CSB

All of us face difficult days. Sometimes even the most devout Christians can become discouraged, and you are no exception. After all, you live in a world where expectations can be high and demands can be even higher.

If you find yourself enduring difficult circumstances, remember that God remains in His heaven. If you become discouraged with the direction of your day or your life, turn your thoughts and prayers to Him. He is a God of possibility, not negativity. He will guide you through your difficulties and beyond them. And then, with a renewed spirit of optimism and hope, you can thank the Giver of all things good for gifts that are simply too numerous to count.

Even in the winter, even in the midst of the storm, the sun is still there. Somewhere, up above the clouds, it still shines and warms and pulls at the life buried deep inside the brown branches and frozen earth.
The sun is there! Spring will come.

Gloria Gaither

When life is difficult, God wants us to have a faith that trusts and waits.

Kay Arthur

The strengthening of faith comes from staying with it in the hour of trial. We should not shrink from tests of faith.

Catherine Marshall

Figuring Out Your Faith: Write down a few of your own ideas about what you should do on difficult days.

_____

_____

_____

_____

Remember That God Wants You to Be a Humble Disciple

He has told you men what is good and what it is the Lord requires of you: Only to act justly, to love faithfulness, and to walk humbly with your God.

Micah 6:8 Holman CSB

When Jesus addressed His disciples, He warned that each one must, "take up his cross and follow me." The disciples must have known exactly what the Master meant. In Jesus' day, prisoners were forced to carry their own crosses to the location where they would be put to death. Thus, Christ's message was clear: in order to follow Him, Christ's disciples must deny themselves and, instead, trust Him completely. Nothing has changed since then.

If we are to be disciples of Christ, we must trust Him and place Him at the very center of our beings. Jesus never comes "next." He is always first.

Do you seek to be a worthy disciple of Christ? Then pick up His cross today and every day that you live. When you do, He will bless you now and forever.

Discipleship is a daily discipline: we follow Jesus
a step at a time, a day at a time.

Warren Wiersbe

Discipleship is a decision to live by what I know about
God, not by what I feel about him or
myself or my neighbors.

Eugene Peterson

Discipleship means allegiance to the suffering Christ,
and it is therefore not at all surprising
that Christians should be called upon to suffer.

Dietrich Bonhoeffer

Figuring Out Your Faith: Write down a few of your
own ideas about what it means to be a disciple.

_____

_____

_____

_____

_____

To Live the Life God Wants You to Live, You Should Learn to Control Your Temper

*My dear brothers and sisters, be quick to listen,
slow to speak, and slow to get angry.
Your anger can never make things right in God's sight.*

James 1:19-20 NLT

Temper tantrums are usually unproductive, unattractive, unforgettable, and unnecessary. Perhaps that's why Proverbs 16:32 states that, "Controlling your temper is better than capturing a city" (NCV).

If you've allowed anger to become a regular visitor at your house, you should pray for wisdom, for patience, and for a heart that is so filled with forgiveness that it contains no room for bitterness. God will help you terminate your tantrums if you ask Him to—and that's a good thing because anger and peace cannot coexist in the same mind.

If you permit yourself to throw too many tantrums, you will forfeit—at least for now—the peace that might otherwise be yours through Christ. So obey God's Word by turning away from anger today and every day. You'll be glad you did, and so will your family and friends.

Life is too short to spend it being angry, bored, or dull.

Barbara Johnson

Anger unresolved will only bring you woe.

Kay Arthur

Anger is the noise of the soul; the unseen irritant of the heart; the relentless invader of silence.

Max Lucado

When you strike out in anger, you may miss the other person, but you will always hit yourself.

Jim Gallery

Figuring Out Your Faith: Write down a few of your own ideas about the value of controlling your temper.

_____

_____

_____

_____

Remember That It Pays to Forgive

You have heard that it was said, You shall love your neighbor and hate your enemy. But I tell you, love your enemies, and pray for those who persecute you.

Matthew 5:43-44 Holman CSB

It has been said that life is an exercise in forgiveness. How true. Christ understood the importance of forgiveness when He commanded, "Love your enemies and pray for those who persecute you" (Matthew 5:43-44 NIV). But sometimes, forgiveness is difficult indeed.

When we have been injured or embarrassed, we feel the urge to strike back and to hurt the one who has hurt us. Christ instructs us to do otherwise. Believers are taught that forgiveness is God's way and that mercy is an integral part of God's plan for our lives. In short, we are commanded to weave the thread of forgiveness into the very fabric of our lives.

Today, as you go about your daily affairs, remember that you have already been forgiven by your Heavenly Father, and so, too, should you forgive others. If you bear bitterness against anyone, take your bitterness to God and leave it there. If you are angry, pray for God's healing hand to calm your spirit. If you are troubled by some past injustice, read God's Word and remember His commandment to forgive. When you follow that commandment and sincerely forgive those who have hurt you, you'll discover that a heavy burden has been lifted from your shoulders. And, you'll discover that although forgiveness is indeed difficult, with God's help, all things are possible.

> Learning how to forgive and forget is one of the secrets of a happy Christian life.
>
> Warren Wiersbe

Figuring Out Your Faith: Write down a few of your own ideas about forgiveness.

_____

_____

_____

_____

_____

Remember That It's Important to Dream Big Dreams

I can do everything through him that gives me strength.

Philippians 4:13 NIV

It takes courage to dream big dreams. You will discover that courage when you do three things: accept the past, trust God to handle the future, and make the most of the time He has given you today.

Are you excited about the opportunities of today and thrilled by the possibilities of tomorrow? Do you confidently expect God to lead you to a place of abundance, peace, and joy? And, when your days on earth are over, do you expect to receive the priceless gift of eternal life? If you trust God's promises, and if you have welcomed God's Son into your heart, then you should believe that your future is intensely and eternally bright.

No dreams are too big for God—not even yours. So start living—and dreaming—accordingly.

You cannot out-dream God.

John Eldredge

Always stay connected to people and seek out things
that bring you joy. Dream with abandon.
Pray confidently.

Barbara Johnson

The future lies all before us. Shall it only be a slight
advance upon what we usually do? Ought it not to be
a bound, a leap forward to altitudes of endeavor
and success undreamed of before?

Annie Armstrong

Figuring Out Your Faith: Write down a few of your
own ideas about the value of aiming high.

_____

_____

_____

_____

_____

Remember That God Wants You to Be Generous

Freely you have received, freely give.

Matthew 10:8 NIV

God's gifts are beyond description, His blessings beyond comprehension. God has been incredibly generous with us, and He rightfully expects us to be generous with others. That's why the thread of generosity is woven into the very fabric of God's teachings.

In the Old Testament, we are told that, "The good person is generous and lends lavishly . . . ." (Psalm 112:5 MSG). And in the New Testament we are instructed, "Freely you have received, freely give" (Matthew 10:8 NKJV). These principles still apply. As we establish priorities for our days and our lives, we are advised to give freely of our time, our possessions, and our love—just as God has given freely to us.

Of course, we can never fully repay God for His gifts, but we can share them with others. And we should.

The measure of a life, after all, is not its duration
but its donation.

Corrie ten Boom

Nothing is really ours until we share it.

C. S. Lewis

A happy spirit takes the grind out of giving.
The grease of gusto frees the gears of generosity.

Charles Swindoll

The mind grows by taking in,
but the heart grows by giving out.

Warren Wiersbe

Figuring Out Your Faith: Write down a few of your
own ideas about ways you can be more generous.

_____

_____

_____

_____

_____

It Pays to Understand the Power of Encouragement

Pleasant words are like a honeycomb,
Sweetness to the soul and health to the bones.

Proverbs 16:24 NKJV

L ife is a team sport, and all of us need occasional pats on the back from our teammates. As Christians, we are called upon to spread the Good News of Christ, and we are also called to spread a message of encouragement and hope to the world.

Whether you realize it or not, many people with whom you come in contact every day are in desperate need of a smile or an encouraging word. The world can be a difficult place, and countless friends and family members may be troubled by the challenges of everyday life. Since you don't always know who needs our help, the best strategy is to try to encourage all the people who cross your path. So today, be a world-class source of encouragement to everyone you meet. Never has the need been greater.

We can never untangle all the woes in other people's lives.
We can't produce miracles overnight.
But we can bring a cup of cool water to a thirsty soul,
or a scoop of laughter to a lonely heart.

Barbara Johnson

How many people stop because so few say, "Go!"

Charles Swindoll

God grant that we may not hinder those who
are battling their way slowly into the light.

Oswald Chambers

Figuring Out Your Faith: Write down a few of your
own ideas about the value of encouragement.

_____

_____

_____

_____

_____

When Your Faith Is Tested, Never Hesitate to Ask God for Help

*And yet the reason you don't have what you want
is that you don't ask God for it.*

James 4:2 Holman CSB

Sometimes, amid the stresses and the frustrations of daily life, we forget to slow ourselves down long enough to talk with God. Instead of turning our thoughts and prayers to Him, we rely entirely upon our own resources, with decidely mixed results. Or, instead of praying for strength, we seek to manufacture it within ourselves, only to find that lasting strength remains elusive.

Are you in need? Ask God to sustain you. And while you're in the mood to ask, don't be afraid to ask for the loving support of your family and friends. When you ask for help, you're likely to receive it. But if you're unwilling to ask, why should you expect to receive it?

So the next time times get tough, remember that help is on the way . . . all you must do is ask.

When will we realize that we're not troubling God with our questions and concerns? His heart is open to hear us— his touch nearer than our next thought—as if no one in the world existed but us. Our very personal God wants to hear from us personally.

Gigi Graham Tchividjian

God will help us become the people we are meant to be, if only we will ask Him.

Hannah Whitall Smith

When trials come your way—as inevitably they will— do not run away. Run to your God and Father.

Kay Arthur

Figuring Out Your Faith: Write down a few of your own ideas about when you should ask God for help.

_____

_____

_____

_____

Remember That Envy Puts Distance Between You and God

Therefore, laying aside all malice, all deceit, hypocrisy, envy, and all evil speaking, as newborn babes, desire the pure milk of the word, that you may grow thereby.

I Peter 2:1-2 NKJV

Because we are frail, imperfect human beings, we are sometimes envious of others. But God's Word warns us that envy is sin. Thus, we must guard ourselves against the natural tendency to feel resentment and jealousy when other people experience good fortune. As believers, we have absolutely no reason to be envious of any people on earth. After all, as Christians we are already recipients of the greatest gift in all creation: God's grace. We have been promised the gift of eternal life through God's only begotten Son, and we must count that gift as our most precious possession.

So here's a simple suggestion that is guaranteed to bring you happiness: fill your heart with God's love, God's promises, and God's Son . . . and when you do so, leave no room for envy, hatred, bitterness, or regret.

How can you possess the miseries of envy when you possess in Christ the best of all portions?

C. H. Spurgeon

Is there somebody who's always getting your goat?
Talk to the Shepherd.

Anonymous

What God asks, does, or requires of others is not my business; it is His.

Kay Arthur

Discontent dries up the soul.

Elisabeth Elliot

Figuring Out Your Faith: Write down a few of your own ideas about the destructive power of envy.

_____

_____

_____

_____

_____

Remember That God Wants You to Be a Good Example

*For am I now trying to win the favor of people, or God?
Or am I striving to please people? If I were still trying to
please people, I would not be a slave of Christ.*

Galatians 1:10 Holman CSB

How do people know that you're a Christian? Well, you can tell them, of course. And make no mistake about it: talking about your faith in God is a very good thing to do. But simply telling people about Jesus isn't enough. You must also be willing to show people how a faithful Christian (like you) should behave.

Whether you like it or not, you simply can't deny the fact that you're an example to other people. The question is not whether you will be an example to your family and friends; the question is precisely what kind of example will you be.

Corrie ten Boom advised, "Don't worry about what you do not understand. Worry about what you do understand in the Bible but do not live by." And that's sound advice because your family, friends, and dates are always watching . . . and so, for that matter, is God.

Too many Christians have geared their program to please,
to entertain, and to gain favor from this world.
We are concerned with how much, instead of how little,
like this age we can become.

Billy Graham

Nothing speaks louder or more powerfully
than a life of integrity.

Charles Swindoll

In your desire to share the gospel,
you may be the only Jesus someone else will ever meet.
Be real and be involved with people.

Barbara Johnson

Figuring Out Your Faith: Write down a few of your
own ideas about what it means to be a good
example.

_____

_____

_____

_____

Faith Helps You Claim God's Abundance

*I have come that they may have life,
and that they may have it more abundantly.*

John 10:10 NKJV

When Jesus talks of the abundant life, is He talking about material riches or earthly fame? Hardly. The Son of God came to this world, not to give it prosperity, but to give it salvation. Thankfully for Christians, our Savior's abundance is both spiritual and eternal; it never falters—even if we do—and it never dies. We need only to open our hearts to Him, and His grace becomes ours.

God's gifts are available to all, but they are not guaranteed; those gifts must be claimed by those who choose to follow Christ. As believers, we are free to accept God's gifts, or not; that choice, and the consequences that result from it, are ours and ours alone.

As we go about our daily lives, may we accept God's promise of spiritual abundance, and may we share it with a world in desperate need of the Master's healing touch.

If we just give God the little that we have,
we can trust Him to make it go around.

Gloria Gaither

If we were given all we wanted here, our hearts would
settle for this world rather than the next.

Elisabeth Elliot

God is the giver, and we are the receivers.
And His richest gifts are bestowed not upon those who do
the greatest things, but upon those who accept
His abundance and His grace.

Hannah Whitall Smith

Figuring Out Your Faith: Write down a few of your
own ideas about ways you can receive God's
abundance.

_____

_____

_____

_____

Bitterness Puts Distance Between You and God

All bitterness, anger and wrath, insult and slander must be removed from you, along with all wickedness. And be kind and compassionate to one another, forgiving one another, just as God also forgave you in Christ.

Ephesians 4:31-32 Holman CSB

If you're unwilling to forgive other people, you're building a roadblock between yourself and God. And the less you're willing to forgive, the bigger your roadblock. So if you want to know God in a more meaningful way, you must learn how to forgive and, to the best of your abilities, forget.

Is there someone out there you need to forgive? If so, pray for that person. And then pray for yourself by asking God to heal your heart. Don't expect forgiveness to be easy or quick, but rest assured: with God as your partner, you can forgive . . . and you will.

By not forgiving, by not letting wrongs go,
we aren't getting back at anyone. We are merely
punishing ourselves by barricading our own hearts.

Jim Cymbala

He who cannot forgive others breaks the bridge
over which he himself must pass.

Corrie ten Boom

Forgiveness enables you to bury your grudge in icy earth.
To put the past behind you. To flush resentment away by
being the first to forgive. Forgiveness fashions your future.
It is a brave and brash thing to do.

Barbara Johnson

Figuring Out Your Faith: Write down a few of your
own ideas about how bitterness impacts your faith.

_____

_____

_____

_____

_____

Remember That It Pays to Be a Cheerful Christian

A cheerful heart has a continual feast.

Proverbs 15:15 Holman CSB

Few things in life are more sad, or, for that matter, more absurd, than a grumpy Christian. Christ promises us lives of abundance and joy, but He does not force His joy upon us. We must claim His joy for ourselves, and when we do, Jesus, in turn, fills our spirits with His power and His love.

How can we receive from Christ the joy that is rightfully ours? By giving Him what is rightfully His: our hearts and our souls.

When we earnestly commit ourselves to the Savior of mankind, when we place Jesus at the center of our lives and trust Him as our personal Savior, He will transform us, not just for today, but for all eternity. Then we, as God's children, can share Christ's joy and His message with a world that needs both.

Be assured, my dear friend, that it is no joy to God
in seeing you with a dreary countenance.

C. H. Spurgeon

The people whom I have seen succeed best in life have
always been cheerful and hopeful people who went
about their business with a smile on their faces.

Charles Kingsley

Christ can put a spring in your step and a thrill
in your heart. Optimism and cheerfulness
are products of knowing Christ.

Billy Graham

Figuring Out Your Faith: Write down a few of your
own ideas about what it means to be a cheerful
Christian.

_____

_____

_____

_____

When Your Faith Is Tested, Learn from Your Mistakes

If you hide your sins, you will not succeed.
If you confess and reject them, you will receive mercy.
Proverbs 28:13 NCV

Everybody makes mistakes, and so will you. In fact, Winston Churchill once observed, "Success is going from failure to failure without loss of enthusiasm." What was good for Churchill is also good for you. You should expect to make mistakes—plenty of mistakes—but you should not allow those missteps to rob you of the enthusiasm you need to fulfill God's plan for your life.

We are imperfect people living in an imperfect world; mistakes are simply part of the price we pay for being here. But, even though mistakes are an inevitable part of life's journey, repeated mistakes should not be. When we commit the inevitable blunders of life, we must correct them, learn from them, and pray for the wisdom not to repeat them. When we do, our mistakes become lessons, and our lives become adventures in growth, not stagnation.

Have you made a mistake or three? Of course you have. But here's the big question: have you used your mistakes as stumbling blocks or stepping stones? The answer to that question will determine how well you will perform in every aspect of your life.

Mistakes offer the possibility for redemption and a new start in God's kingdom. No matter what you're guilty of, God can restore your innocence.

Barbara Johnson

Very few things motivate us to give God our undivided attention like being faced with the negative consequences of our decisions.

Charles Stanley

Figuring Out Your Faith: Write down a few of your own ideas about the best way to handle mistakes.

_____

_____

_____

_____

_____

Remember That Negativity Is a Trap

Let angry people endure the backlash of their own anger;
if you try to make it better, you'll only make it worse.

Proverbs 19:19 MSG

From experience, we know that it is easy to criticize others. And we know that it is usually far easier to find faults than to find solutions. Still, the urge to criticize others remains a powerful temptation for most of us.

Negativity is highly contagious: We give it to others who, in turn, give it back to us. This stress-inducing cycle can be broken only by positive thoughts, heartfelt prayers, encouraging words, and meaningful acts of kindness.

As thoughtful servants of a loving God, we have no valid reason—and no legitimate excuse—to be negative. So, when we are tempted to be overly critical of others, or unfairly critical of ourselves, we must use the transforming power of God's love to break the chains of negativity. We must defeat negativity before negativity defeats us.

Winners see an answer for every problem;
losers see a problem in every answer.

Barbara Johnson

We never get anywhere—nor do our conditions
and circumstances change—when we look
at the dark side of life.

Mrs. Charles E. Cowman

To lose heart is to lose everything.

John Eldredge

After one hour in heaven,
we shall be ashamed that we ever grumbled.

Vance Havner

Figuring Out Your Faith: Write down a few of your
own ideas about how negativity impacts your faith.

_____

_____

_____

_____

_____

Remember That It Pays to Be Patient

Be gentle to everyone, able to teach, and patient.

2 Timothy 2:23 Holman CSB

Are you a perfectly patient person? If so, feel free to skip the rest of this page. But if you're not, here's something to think about: If you really want to become a more patient person, God is ready and willing to help.

The Bible promises that when you sincerely seek God's help, He will give you the things that you need—and that includes patience. But God won't force you to become a more patient person. If you want to become a more mature Christian, you've got to do some of the work yourself—and the best time to start doing that work is now.

So, if you want to gain patience and maturity, bow your head and start praying about it. Then, rest assured that with God's help, you can most certainly make yourself a more patient, understanding, mature Christian.

As we wait on God, He helps us use the winds of adversity
to soar above our problems. As the Bible says,
"Those who wait on the LORD . . .
shall mount up with wings like eagles."

Billy Graham

You can't step in front of God and not get in trouble.
When He says, "Go three steps," don't go four.

Charles Stanley

Be patient. God is using today's difficulties to strengthen
you for tomorrow. He is equipping you.
The God who makes things grow will help you bear fruit.

Max Lucado

Figuring Out Your Faith: Write down a few of your
own ideas about the value of patience.

_____

_____

_____

_____

_____

Remember That God Offers Peace

These things I have spoken to you, that in Me you may have peace. In the world you will have tribulation; but be of good cheer, I have overcome the world.

John 16:33 NKJV

Oftentimes, our outer struggles are simply manifestations of the inner conflict that we feel when we stray from God's path. Jesus offers us peace, not as the world gives, but as He alone gives. Our challenge is to accept Christ's peace into our hearts and then, as best we can, to share His peace with our neighbors. When we accept Jesus as our personal Savior, we are transformed by His grace. We are then free to accept the spiritual abundance and peace that can be ours through the power of the risen Christ.

Have you found the genuine peace that can be yours through Jesus Christ? Or are you still rushing after the illusion of "peace and happiness" that the world promises but cannot deliver? Today, as a gift to yourself, to your family, and to your friends, claim the inner peace that is your spiritual birthright: the peace of Jesus Christ. It is offered freely;

it has been paid for in full; it is yours for the asking. So ask. And then share.

> Prayer guards hearts and minds and causes
> God to bring peace out of chaos.
>
> Beth Moore

> The fruit of our placing all things in God's hands is
> the presence of His abiding peace in our hearts.
>
> Hannah Whitall Smith

> When we do what is right, we have contentment,
> peace, and happiness.
>
> Beverly LaHaye

Figuring Out Your Faith: Write down a few of your own ideas about ways to find God's peace.

_____

_____

_____

_____

_____

To Strengthen Your Faith, You Should Avoid the Wrong Kind of Peer Pressure

Whoever walks with the wise will become wise;
whoever walks with fools will suffer harm.
Proverbs 13:20 NLT

Who you are depends, to a surprising extent, on the people you hang out with. Peer pressure can be good or bad, depending upon who your peers are and how they behave. If your friends encourage you to follow God's will and to obey His commandments, then you'll experience positive peer pressure, and that's a good thing. But, if your friends encourage you to do foolish things, then you're facing a different kind of peer pressure . . . and you'd better beware.

Do you want to feel good about yourself and your life? If so, here's a simple, proven strategy: go out and find friends who, by their words and their actions, will help you build the kind of life that's worth feeling good about.

Nothing can be more dangerous than keeping wicked companions. They communicate the infection of their vices to all who associate with them.

St. Jean Baptiste de la Salle

Choose the opposition of the whole world rather than offend Jesus.

Thomas à Kempis

When we are set free from the bondage of pleasing others, when we are free from currying others' favor and others' approval—then no one will be able to make us miserable or dissatisfied. And then, if we know we have pleased God, contentment will be our consolation.

Kay Arthur

Figuring Out Your Faith: Write down a few of your own ideas about avoiding the wrong kind of peer pressure.

_____

_____

_____

_____

Remember That Good Decisions Pay Big Dividends

If you need wisdom—if you want to know what God wants you to do—ask him, and he will gladly tell you. He will not resent your asking.

James 1:5 NLT

Everyday life is an adventure in decision-making. Each day, we make countless decisions that hopefully bring us closer to God. When we obey God's commandments, we share in His abundance and His peace. But, when we turn our backs upon God by disobeying Him, we invite Old Man Trouble to stop by for an extended visit.

Do you want to be successful, satisfied, and happy with the direction of your life? If so, here's a good place to start: Obey God. When you're faced with a difficult choice or a powerful temptation, pray about it. Invite God into your heart and live according to His commandments. When you do, you will be blessed today, and tomorrow, and forever.

If we don't hunger and thirst after righteousness,
we'll become anemic and feel miserable in
our Christian experience.

Franklin Graham

Righteousness not only defines God,
but God defines righteousness.

Bill Hybels

Life is built on character,
but character is built on decisions.

Warren Wiersbe

Figuring Out Your Faith: Write down a few of your
own ideas about ways to make better decisions.

_____

_____

_____

_____

_____

Always Remember That God Answers Prayers

If you believe, you will receive whatever you ask for in prayer.

Matthew 21:22 NIV

In case you've been wondering, wonder no more—God does answer your prayers. What God does not do is this: He does not always answer your prayers as soon as you might like, and He does not always answer your prayers by saying "Yes."

God isn't an order-taker, and He's not some sort of cosmic vending machine. Sometimes—even when we want something very badly—our loving Heavenly Father responds to our requests by saying "No," and we must accept His answer, even if we don't understand it.

God answers prayers not only according to our wishes but also according to His master plan. We cannot know that plan, but we can know the Planner . . . and we must trust His wisdom, His righteousness, and His love.

Of this you can be sure: God is listening, and He wants to hear from you now. So what are you waiting for?

Avail yourself of the greatest privilege this side of heaven: prayer. Jesus Christ died to make this communion and communication with the Father possible.

Billy Graham

When you ask God to do something, don't ask timidly; put your whole heart into it.

Marie T. Freeman

Are you weak? Weary? Confused? Troubled? Pressured? How is your relationship with God? Is it held in its place of priority? I believe the greater the pressure, the greater your need for time alone with Him.

Kay Arthur

Figuring Out Your Faith: Write down a few of your own ideas about your prayer life.

_____

_____

_____

_____

_____

Remember That God Is Sufficient to Meet All Your Needs

The Lord is my rock, my fortress, and my deliverer.

Psalm 18:2 Holman CSB

It is easy to become overwhelmed by the demands of everyday life, but if you're a faithful follower of the One from Galilee, you need never be overwhelmed. Why? Because God's love is sufficient to meet your needs. Whatever dangers you may face, whatever heartbreaks you must endure, God is with you, and He stands ready to comfort you and to heal you.

The Psalmist writes, "Weeping may endure for a night, but joy comes in the morning" (Psalm 30:5 NKJV). But when we are suffering, the morning may seem very far away. It is not. God promises that He is "near to those who have a broken heart" (Psalm 34:18 NKJV).

If you are experiencing the intense pain of a recent loss, or if you are still mourning a loss from long ago, perhaps you are now ready to begin the next stage of your journey with God. If so, be mindful of this fact: the loving heart of God is sufficient to meet any challenge, including yours.

God is always sufficient in perfect proportion to our need.
Beth Moore

God is, must be, our answer to every question
and every cry of need.
Hannah Whitall Smith

God will call you to obey Him and do whatever He asks of
you. However, you do not need to be doing something to
feel fulfilled. You are fulfilled completely in a relationship
with God. When you are filled with Him,
what else do you need?
Henry Blackaby and Claude King

Figuring Out Your Faith: Write down a few of your
own ideas about God's sufficiency.

_____

_____

_____

_____

_____

Remember That It's Important to Be Courteous

Be hospitable to one another without grumbling.

I Peter 4:9 NKJV

Did Christ instruct us in matters of etiquette and courtesy? Of course He did. Christ's instructions are clear: "In everything, therefore, treat people the same way you want them to treat you, for this is the Law and the Prophets" (Matthew 7:12 NASB). Jesus did not say, "In some things, treat people as you wish to be treated." And, He did not say, "From time to time, treat others with kindness." Christ said that we should treat others as we wish to be treated in every aspect of our daily lives. This, of course, is a tall order indeed, but as Christians, we are commanded to do our best.

Today, be a little kinder than necessary to family members, friends, and total strangers. And, as you consider all the things that Christ has done in your life, honor Him with your words and with your deeds. He expects no less, and He deserves no less.

When you extend hospitality to others, you're not trying
to impress people; you're trying to reflect God to them.

Max Lucado

Only the courteous can love,
but it is love that makes them courteous.

C. S. Lewis

Courtesy is contagious.

Marie T. Freeman

If you are willing to honor a person out of respect for God,
you can be assured that God will honor you.

Beth Moore

Figuring Out Your Faith: Write down a few of your
own ideas about the value of courtesy.

_____

_____

_____

_____

_____

Remember That God Can Renew Your Strength

He gives strength to the weary and strengthens the powerless.

Isaiah 40:29 Holman CSB

When we genuinely lift our hearts and prayers to God, He renews our strength. Are you almost too stressed to lift your head? Then bow it. Offer your concerns and your fears to your Father in heaven. He is always at your side, offering His love and His strength.

Are you troubled or anxious? Take your anxieties to God in prayer. Are you weak or worried? Delve deeply into God's Holy Word and sense His presence in the quiet moments of the day. Are you spiritually exhausted? Call upon fellow believers to support you, and call upon Christ to renew your spirit and your life. Your Savior will never let you down. To the contrary, He will always lift you up if you ask Him to. So what, dear friend, are you waiting for?

He is the God of wholeness and restoration.

Stormie Omartian

Repentance removes old sins and wrong attitudes,
and it opens the way for the Holy Spirit to restore
our spiritual health.

Shirley Dobson

When we reach the end of our strength, wisdom,
and personal resources, we enter
into the beginning of his glorious provisions.

Patsy Clairmont

Figuring Out Your Faith: Write down a few of your
own ideas about ways to renew your strength.

_____

_____

_____

_____

_____

Have Faith in Your Future

"I say this because I know what I am planning for you,"
says the Lord. "I have good plans for you, not plans to hurt
you. I will give you hope and a good future."

Jeremiah 29:11 NCV

How can you make smart choices if you're unwilling to trust God and obey Him? The answer, of course, is that you can't. That's why you should trust God in everything (and that means entrusting your future to God).

How bright is your future? Well, if you're a faithful believer, God's plans for you are so bright that you'd better wear shades. But here are some important follow-up questions: How bright do you believe your future to be? Are you expecting a terrific tomorrow, or are you dreading a terrible one? The answer you give will have a powerful impact on the way tomorrow turns out.

Do you trust in the ultimate goodness of God's plan for your life? Will you face tomorrow's challenges with optimism and hope? You should. After all, God created you for a very important reason: His reason. And you have important work to do: His work.

Today, as you live in the present and look to the future, remember that God has an amazing plan for you. Act—and believe—accordingly.

We must trust as if it all depended on God and work
as if it all depended on us.

C. H. Spurgeon

Every man lives by faith, the nonbeliever as well as
the saint; the one by faith in natural laws and the other by
faith in God.

A. W. Tozer

The Christian believes in a fabulous future.

Billy Graham

Figuring Out Your Faith: Write down a few of your
own ideas about entrusting the future to God.

_____

_____

_____

_____

_____

Remember to Put the Brakes on Impulsivity

I will instruct you and teach you in the way you should go;
I will guide you with My eye.

Psalm 32:8 NKJV

Maybe you've heard this old saying: "Look before you leap." Well, that saying may be old, but it still applies to you. Before you jump into something, you should look ahead and plan ahead. Otherwise, you might soon be sorry you jumped!

When you acquire the habit of thinking ahead and planning ahead, you'll make better choices (and, as a result, you'll feel better about yourself).

So when it comes to the important things in life, don't allow impulsive behavior to dynamite your future. Think long and hard about the consequences of your actions before you do something foolish . . . or dangerous . . . or both.

It's incredible to realize that what we do each day has meaning in the big picture of God's plan.

Bill Hybels

Allow your dreams a place in your prayers and plans. God-given dreams can help you move into the future He is preparing for you.

Barbara Johnson

The only way you can experience abundant life is to surrender your plans to Him.

Charles Stanley

Figuring Out Your Faith: Write down a few of your own ideas about the dangers of being too impulsive.

_____

_____

_____

_____

Remember That God Wants You to Use Your Gifts

I remind you to keep ablaze the gift of God that is in you.

2 Timothy 1:6 Holman CSB

How do we thank God for the gifts He has given us? By using those gifts, that's how!

God has given you talents and opportunities that are uniquely yours. Are you willing to use your gifts in the way that God intends? And are you willing to summon the discipline that is required to develop your talents and to hone your skills? That's precisely what God wants you to do, and that's precisely what you should desire for yourself.

As you seek to expand your talents, you will undoubtedly encounter stumbling blocks along the way, such as the fear of rejection or the fear of failure. When you do, don't stumble! Just continue to refine your skills, and offer your services to God. And when the time is right, He will use you—but it's up to you to be thoroughly prepared when He does.

You are the only person on earth who can use your ability.

Zig Ziglar

God often reveals His direction for our lives through
the way He made us . . .
with a certain personality and unique skills.

Bill Hybels

God has given you special talents—
now it's your turn to give them back to God.

Marie T. Freeman

Figuring Out Your Faith: Write down a few of your
own ideas about using your gifts.

_____

_____

_____

_____

_____

When You Figure Out Your Faith, You Can Move Mountains

For I assure you: If you have faith the size of a mustard seed, you will tell this mountain, "Move from here to there," and it will move. Nothing will be impossible for you.

Matthew 17:20 Holman CSB

Because we live in a demanding world, all of us have mountains to climb and mountains to move. Moving those mountains requires faith.

Are you a mountain-moving Christian whose faith is evident for all to see? Or, are you a spiritual underachiever? As you think about the answer to that question, consider this: God needs more people who are willing to move mountains for His glory and for His kingdom.

Are you willing to let God help you move mountains, or are you still stumbling around over a few little molehills? The answer should be obvious. And so, with no more delays, let the mountain moving begin.

A faith that hasn't been tested can't be trusted.

Adrian Rogers

Faith never knows where it is being led,
but it loves and knows the One Who is leading.

Oswald Chambers

Great hopes make great men.

Thomas Fuller

We are never stronger than the moment
we admit we are weak.

Beth Moore

Figuring Out Your Faith: Write down a few of your
own ideas about mountains you need to move.

_____

_____

_____

_____

_____

When You Figure Out Your Faith, You'll Understand That God's Truth Is the Ultimate Truth

You will know the truth, and the truth will set you free.

John 8:32 Holman CSB

God is vitally concerned with truth. His Word teaches the truth; His Spirit reveals the truth; His Son leads us to the truth. When we open our hearts to God, and when we allow His Son to rule over our thoughts and our lives, God reveals Himself, and we come to understand the truth about ourselves and the Truth (with a capital T) about God's gift of grace.

The familiar words of John 8:32 remind us that when we come to know God's Truth, we are liberated. Have you been liberated by that Truth? And are you living in accordance with the eternal truths that you find in God's Holy Word? Hopefully so.

Today, as you fulfill the responsibilities that God has placed before you, ask yourself this question: "Do my thoughts and actions bear witness to the ultimate Truth that God has placed in my heart, or am I allowing the pressures of everyday life to overwhelm me?" It's a profound question that deserves an answer . . . now.

Let everything perish! Dismiss these empty vanities!
And let us take up the search for the truth.
St. Augustine

We must go out and live among them, manifesting
the gentle, loving spirit of our Lord.
We need to make friends before we can hope
to make converts.
Lottie Moon

Figuring Out Your Faith: Write down a few of your own ideas about ways you can bear witness to God's truth.

_____

_____

_____

_____

To Strengthen Your Faith, You Should Worship God Every Day

Worship the Lord your God and . . . serve Him only.

Matthew 4:10 Holman CSB

If you really want to know God, you must be willing to worship Him seven days a week, not just on Sunday.

God has a wonderful plan for your life, and an important part of that plan includes the time that you set aside for praise and worship. Every life, including yours, is based upon some form of worship. The question is not whether you will worship, but what you worship.

If you choose to worship God, you will receive a bountiful harvest of joy, peace, and abundance. But if you distance yourself from God by foolishly worshiping earthly possessions and personal gratification, you're making a huge mistake. So do this: Worship God today and every day. Worship Him with sincerity and thanksgiving. Write His name on your heart and rest assured that He, too, has written your name on His.

Worship is a voluntary act of gratitude offered
by the saved to the Savior, by the healed to the Healer,
by the delivered to the Deliverer.

Max Lucado

Worship is spiritual. Our worship must be more than
just outward expression,
it must also take place in our spirits.

Franklin Graham

To worship Him in truth means to worship Him honestly,
without hypocrisy, standing open
and transparent before Him.

Anne Graham Lotz

Figuring Out Your Faith: Write down a few of your
own ideas about worship.

_____

_____

_____

_____

_____

Your Circumstances Change, But God Doesn't

For I am the Lord, I do not change.

Malachi 3:6 NKJV

We live in a world that is always changing, but we worship a God that never changes—thank goodness! That means that we can be comforted in the knowledge that our Heavenly Father is the rock that simply cannot be moved: "I am the Lord, I do not change" (Malachi 3:6 NKJV).

The next time you face difficult circumstances, tough times, unfair treatment, or unwelcome changes, remember that some things never change—things like the love that you feel in your heart for your family and friends . . . and the love that God feels for you. So, instead of worrying too much about life's inevitable challenges, focus your energies on finding solutions. Have faith in your own abilities, do your best to solve your problems, and leave the rest up to God.

The secret of contentment in the midst of change is found
in having roots in the changeless Christ—
the same yesterday, today and forever.

Ed Young

The resurrection of Jesus Christ is the power of God to
change history and to change lives.

Bill Bright

Conditions are always changing; therefore,
I must not be dependent upon conditions.
What matters supremely is my soul
and my relationship to God.

Corrie ten Boom

Figuring Out Your Faith: Write down a few of your
own ideas about change.

_____

_____

_____

_____

_____

To Figure Out Where You're Going, Let God Be Your Guide

The true children of God are those who let God's Spirit lead them.

Romans 8:14 NCV

The Bible promises that God will guide you if you let Him. Your job is to let Him. But sometimes, you will be tempted to do otherwise. Sometimes, you'll be tempted to go along with the crowd; other times, you'll be tempted to do things your way, not God's way. When you feel these temptations, resist them.

God has promised that when you ask for His help, He will not withhold it. So ask. Ask Him to meet the needs of your day. Ask Him to lead you, to protect you, and to correct you. And trust the answers He gives.

God stands at the door and waits. When you knock, He opens. When you ask, He answers. Your task, of course, is to seek His guidance prayerfully, confidently, and often.

We have ample evidence that the Lord is able to guide.
The promises cover every imaginable situation.
All we need to do is to take the hand he stretches out.

Elisabeth Elliot

Only He can guide you to invest your life in
worthwhile ways. This guidance will come as you
"walk" with Him and listen to Him.

Henry Blackaby and Claude King

Are you serious about wanting God's guidance
to become a personal reality in your life? The first step is
to tell God that you know you can't manage your own life;
that you need his help.

Catherine Marshall

Figuring Out Your Faith: Write down a few of your
own ideas about God's guidance.

_____

_____

_____

_____

_____

God Has a Plan for You, and He Wants You to Figure It Out

You will show me the path of life.

Psalm 16:11 NKJV

You'll feel better about yourself if you're living on purpose, not by accident. But sometimes that's hard to do. Why? Because God's plans aren't always clear. Sometimes we wander aimlessly in a wilderness of our own making. And sometimes, we struggle mightily against God in an unsuccessful attempt to find success and happiness through our own means, not His.

Are you genuinely trying to figure out God's purpose for your life? If so, you can be sure that with God's help, you will eventually discover it. So keep praying, and keep watching. And rest assured: God's got big plans for you . . . very big plans.

And when you discover those plans, you'll feel better about yourself . . . lot's better.

God is preparing you as his chosen arrow. As yet your shaft is hidden in his quiver, in the shadows, but, at the precise moment, he will reach for you and launch you to that place of his appointment.

Charles Swindoll

When the dream of our heart is one that God has planted there, a strange happiness flows into us. At that moment, all of the spiritual resources of the universe are released to help us. Our praying is then at one with the will of God and becomes a channel for the Creator's purposes for us and our world.

Catherine Marshall

Figuring Out Your Faith: Write down a few of your own ideas about God's plan.

_____

_____

_____

_____

_____

Remember That God Works Miracles

Is anything too hard for the LORD?

Genesis 18:14 KJV

Is your faith a little threadbare and worn? If so, it's time to abandon your doubts and reclaim your faith in God's promises.

Ours is a God of infinite possibilities. But sometimes, because of limited faith and limited understanding, we wrongly assume that God cannot or will not intervene in the affairs of mankind. Such assumptions are simply wrong.

God's Holy Word makes it clear: absolutely nothing is impossible for the Lord. And since the Bible means what it says, you can be comforted in the knowledge that the Creator of the universe can do miraculous things in your own life and in the lives of your loved ones. Your challenge, as a believer, is to take God at His word, and to expect the miraculous.

If we take God's program, we can have God's power—
not otherwise.

E. Stanley Jones

You can believe in the Holy Spirit not because you see
Him, but because you see what He does in people's lives
when they are surrendered to Christ
and possess His power.

Billy Graham

No giant will ever be a match for a big God
with a little rock.

Beth Moore

Figuring Out Your Faith: Write down a few of your
own ideas about God's power.

_____

_____

_____

_____

_____

Genuine Faith Is Humble Faith

*Therefore humble yourselves under the mighty hand of God,
that He may exalt you in due time.*

I Peter 5:6 NKJV

On the road to spiritual growth, pride is a massive roadblock. The more prideful you are, the more difficult it is to know God. When you experience success, it's easy to puff out your chest and proclaim, "I did that!" But it's wrong. Dietrich Bonhoeffer was correct when he observed, "It is very easy to overestimate the importance of our own achievements in comparison with what we owe others." In other words, reality breeds humility. So if you want to know God better, be humble. Otherwise, you'll be building a roadblock between you and your Creator (and that's a very bad thing to do!).

Do you wish to rise? Begin by descending.
You plan a tower that will pierce the clouds?
Lay first the foundation of humility.

St. Augustine

The great characteristic of the saint is humility.

Oswald Chambers

Nothing sets a person so much out of
the devil's reach as humility.

Jonathan Edwards

We are never stronger than the moment
we admit we are weak.

Beth Moore

Figuring Out Your Faith: Write down a few of your
own ideas about the need to stay humble.

_____

_____

_____

_____

_____

To Build Your Faith, Keep Looking for Miracles

God verified the message by signs and wonders and various miracles and by giving gifts of the Holy Spirit whenever he chose to do so.

Hebrews 2:4 NLT

One way we can strengthen our faith is by looking carefully at the miraculous things that God does. But sometimes, we're simply too preoccupied to notice. Instead of paying careful attention to God's handiwork, we become distracted. Instead of expecting God to work miracles, we become cynical. Instead of depending on God's awesome power, we seek to muddle along using our own power—with decidedly mixed results.

Miracles, both great and small, are an integral part of everyday life—and they are a part of your life, too. But here's the million-dollar question: have you noticed?

If you lack the faith that God can work miracles in your own life, it's time to reconsider. Instead of doubting God, trust His power, and expect His miracles. Then, wait patiently . . . because something miraculous is about to happen.

Only God can move mountains,
but faith and prayer can move God.

E. M. Bounds

When God is involved, anything can happen.
Be open and stay that way. God has a beautiful way of
bringing good vibrations out of broken chords.

Charles Swindoll

I could go through this day oblivious to the miracles
all around me or I could tune in and "enjoy."

Gloria Gaither

Figuring Out Your Faith: Write down a few of your
own ideas about miracles.

_____

_____

_____

_____

_____

Remember That God's Protection Is the Ultimate Armor

If God is for us, who can be against us?

Romans 8:31 NIV

God has promised to protect us, and He intends to keep His promise. In a world filled with dangers and temptations, God is the ultimate armor. In a world filled with misleading messages, God's Word is the ultimate truth. In a world filled with more frustrations than we can count, God's Son offers the ultimate peace.

Will you accept God's peace and wear God's armor against the dangers of our world? Hopefully so—because when you do, you can live courageously, knowing that you possess the ultimate protection: God's unfailing love for you.

Under heaven's lock and key, we are protected
by the most efficient security system available:
the power of God.

Charles Swindoll

The Rock of Ages is the great sheltering encirclement.

Oswald Chambers

The Will of God will never take you where
the Grace of God will not protect you.

Anonymous

Figuring Out Your Faith: Write down a few of your
own ideas about God's protection.

_____

_____

_____

_____

_____

Remember That
God Rules Over Everything

*Can you understand the secrets of God? His limits are higher
than the heavens; you cannot reach them! They are deeper
than the grave; you cannot understand them! His limits are
longer than the earth and wider than the sea.*

Job 11:7-9 NCV

God reigns over the entire universe and He reigns
over your little corner of that universe. He is sovereign. Your challenge is to recognize God's sovereignty and live in accordance with His commandments.
Sometimes, of course, this is easier said than done.

Your Heavenly Father may not always reveal Himself
as quickly (or as clearly) as you would like. But rest assured:
God is in control, God is here, and God intends to use
you in wonderful, unexpected ways. He desires to lead you
along a path of His choosing. Your challenge is to watch, to
listen, to learn . . . and to follow.

Our God is the sovereign Creator of the universe!
He loves us as His own children and has provided
every good thing we have; He is worthy
of our praise every moment.

Shirley Dobson

The next time you're disappointed, don't panic.
Don't give up. Just be patient and
let God remind you he's still in control.

Max Lucado

God is in control, and therefore in everything I can give
thanks, not because of the situation, but because of the
One who directs and rules over it.

Kay Arthur

Figuring Out Your Faith: Write down a few of your
own ideas about God's sovereignty.

_____

_____

_____

_____

_____

Remember That It Pays to Solve Problems Sooner Rather Than Later

People who do what is right may have many problems, but the Lord will solve them all.

Psalm 34:19 NCV

L ife is an adventure in problem-solving. When it comes to solving the problems of everyday living, we often know precisely what needs to be done, but we may be slow in doing it—especially if what needs to be done is difficult. So we put off till tomorrow what should be done today.

As a young person living here in the 21st century, you have your own set of challenges. As you face those challenges, you may be comforted by this fact: Trouble, of every kind, is temporary. Yet God's grace is eternal. And worries, of every kind, are temporary. But God's love is everlasting. The troubles that concern you will pass. God remains. And for every problem, God has a solution.

The words of Psalm 34 remind us that the Lord solves problems for "people who do what is right." And usually, doing "what is right" means doing the uncomfortable work of confronting our problems sooner rather than later. So with no further ado, let the problem-solving begin . . . right now.

Each problem is a God-appointed instructor.

Charles Swindoll

Life will be made or broken at the place
where we meet and deal with obstacles.

E. Stanley Jones

Figuring Out Your Faith: Write down a few of your own ideas about problems that need solving.

_____

_____

_____

_____

_____

It's Important to Trust God's Timing

He has made everything appropriate in its time.
He has also put eternity in their hearts, but man cannot
discover the work God has done from beginning to end.
Ecclesiastes 3:11 Holman CSB

A re you anxious for God to work out His plan for your life? Who isn't? As believers, we all want God to do great things for us and through us, and we want Him to do those things now. But sometimes, God has other plans. Sometimes, God's timetable does not coincide with our own. It's worth noting, however, that God's timetable is always perfect.

The next time you find your patience tested to the limit, remember that the world unfolds according to God's plan, not ours. Sometimes, we must wait patiently, and that's as it should be. After all, think how patient God has been with us.

Will not the Lord's time be better than your time?

C. H. Spurgeon

God has a designated time when his promise will be
fulfilled and the prayer will be answered.

Jim Cymbala

When there is perplexity there is always guidance—
not always at the moment we ask, but in good time,
which is God's time. There is no need to fret and stew.

Elisabeth Elliot

Your times are in His hands.
He's in charge of the timetable, so wait patiently.

Kay Arthur

Figuring Out Your Faith: Write down a few of your
own ideas about God's timetable.

_____

_____

_____

_____

_____

Remember That Gossip Is Destructive

*So rid yourselves of all wickedness,
all deceit, hypocrisy, envy, and all slander.*

I Peter 2:1 Holman CSB

Face facts: gossip is the guilty little pleasure that tempts almost all of us from time to time. Why is it so tempting to gossip? Because when we put other people down, we experience a brief dose of self-righteousness as we look down our noses at the misdeeds of others. But there's a catch: in truth, we can never really build ourselves up by tearing other people down. So the habit of gossip turns out to be a self-defeating waste of time.

It's no wonder that the Bible clearly teaches that gossip is wrong. Consider the simple advice found in Proverbs 16:28: "Gossip ruins friendships" (NCV). So do yourself a big favor: don't spend precious time talking about other people. It's a waste of words, it's the wrong thing to do, and in the end, it will leave you with less self-respect, not more.

When you avoid the temptation to engage in gossip, you'll feel better about yourself—and other people will feel better about you, too. So don't do it.

Change the heart, and you change the speech.

Warren Wiersbe

The great test of a man's character is his tongue.

Oswald Chambers

To belittle is to be little.

Anonymous

The cost of gossip always exceeds its worth.

Marie T. Freeman

Figuring Out Your Faith: Write down a few of your own ideas about the dangers of gossip.

_____

_____

_____

_____

_____

DAY 70

To Strengthen Your Faith, Establish Habits That Are Pleasing to God

I, the Lord, examine the mind, I test the heart to give to each according to his way, according to what his actions deserve.

Jeremiah 17:10 Holman CSB

It's an old saying and a true one: First, you make your habits, and then your habits make you. Some habits will inevitably bring you closer to God; other habits will lead you away from the path He has chosen for you. If you sincerely desire to improve your spiritual health, you must honestly examine the habits that make up the fabric of your day. And you must abandon those habits that are displeasing to God.

If you trust God, and if you keep asking for His help, He can transform your life. If you sincerely ask Him to help you, the same God who created the universe will help you defeat the harmful habits that have heretofore defeated you. So, if at first you don't succeed, keep praying. God is listening, and He's ready to help you become a better person if you ask Him . . . so ask today.

You can build up a set of good habits so that you habitually
take the Christian way without thought.

E. Stanley Jones

You will never change your life until you change
something you do daily.

John Maxwell

If you want to form a new habit, get to work.
If you want to break a bad habit, get on your knees.

Marie T. Freeman

Since behaviors become habits, make them work
with you and not against you.

E. Stanley Jones

Figuring Out Your Faith: Write down a few of your
own ideas about habits.

_____

_____

_____

_____

_____

To Strengthen Your Faith, Put Holiness Before Happiness

Blessed are those who hunger and thirst for righteousness, because they will be filled.

Matthew 5:6 Holman CSB

Because you are an imperfect human being, you are not "perfectly" happy—and that's perfectly okay with God. He is far less concerned with your happiness than He is with your holiness.

God continuously reveals Himself in everyday life, but He does not do so in order to make you contented; He does so in order to lead you to His Son. So don't be overly concerned with your current level of happiness; it will change. Be more concerned with the current state of your relationship with Christ: He does not change. And because your Savior transcends time and space, you can be comforted in the knowledge that in the end, His joy will become your joy . . . for all eternity.

You don't have to be like the world to have an impact on the world. You don't have to be like the crowd to change the crowd. You don't have to lower yourself down to their level to lift them up to your level. Holiness doesn't seek to be odd. Holiness seeks to be like God.

Max Lucado

A holy life simply is a life that works.

Richard Foster

Our ultimate aim in life is not to be healthy, wealthy, prosperous, or problem free. Our ultimate aim in life is to bring glory to God.

Anne Graham Lotz

Figuring Out Your Faith: Write down a few of your own ideas about what it means to put holiness before happiness.

_____

_____

_____

_____

To Strengthen Your Faith, Be Careful How You Direct Your Thoughts

Finally brothers, whatever is true, whatever is honorable, whatever is just, whatever is pure, whatever is lovely, whatever is commendable—if there is any moral excellence and if there is any praise—dwell on these things.

Philippians 4:8 Holman CSB

How will you direct your thoughts today? Will you obey the words of Philippians 4:8 by dwelling upon those things that are honorable, true, and worthy of praise? Or will you allow your thoughts to be hijacked by the negativity that seems to dominate our troubled world.

Are you fearful, angry, bored, or worried? Are you so preoccupied with the concerns of this day that you fail to thank God for the promise of eternity? Are you confused, bitter, or pessimistic? If so, God wants to have a little talk with you. He wants to remind you of His infinite love and His boundless grace. As you contemplate these things, and as you give thanks for God's blessings, negativity should no longer dominate your day or your life.

Our own possible bad thoughts and deeds are far more dangerous to us than any enemy from the world.

St. Ambrose

We know well enough how to keep outward silence, and to hush our spoken words, but we know little of interior silence. It consists in hushing our idle, restless, wandering imagination, in quieting the promptings of our worldly minds, and in suppressing the crowd of unprofitable thoughts which excite and disturb the soul.

François Fènelon

People who do not develop and practice good thinking often find themselves at the mercy of their circumstances.

John Maxwell

Figuring Out Your Faith: Write down a few of your own ideas about how your thoughts impact your faith.

_____

_____

_____

_____

Always Remember That God Is Trustworthy

It is better to trust the Lord than to put confidence in people.
It is better to trust the Lord than to put confidence in princes.

Psalm 118:8-9 NLT

Sometimes the future seems bright, and sometimes it does not. Yet even when we cannot see the possibilities of tomorrow, God can. As believers, our challenge is to trust an uncertain future to an all-powerful God.

When we trust God, we should trust Him without reservation. We should steel ourselves against the inevitable stresses of the day, secure in the knowledge that our Heavenly Father has a plan for the future that only He can see.

Can you place your future into the hands of a loving and all-knowing God? Can you live amid the uncertainties of today, knowing that God has dominion over all your tomorrows? If you can, you are wise and you are blessed. When you trust God with everything you are and everything you have, He will bless you now and forever.

Conditions are always changing; therefore, I must not be dependent upon conditions. What matters supremely is my soul and my relationship to God.

Corrie ten Boom

Sometimes the very essence of faith is trusting God in the midst of things He knows good and well we cannot comprehend.

Beth Moore

Are you serious about wanting God's guidance to become the person he wants you to be?
The first step is to tell God that you know you can't manage your own life; that you need his help.

Catherine Marshall

Figuring Out Your Faith: Write down a few of your own ideas about trusting God.

_____

_____

_____

_____

_____

When Your Faith Is Tested, Cast Your Burdens on the Lord, and You'll Be Victorious

Cast your burden upon the Lord and He will sustain you:
He will never allow the righteous to be shaken.
Psalm 55:22 NASB

Your decision to seek a deeper relationship with God will not remove all problems from your life; to the contrary, it will bring about a series of personal crises as you constantly seek to say "yes" to God although the world encourages you to do otherwise. You live in a world that seeks to snare your attention and lead you away from God. Each time you are tempted to distance yourself from the Creator, you will face a spiritual crisis. A few of these crises may be monumental in scope, but most will be the small, everyday decisions of life. In fact, life here on earth can be seen as one test after another—and with each crisis comes yet another opportunity to grow closer to God . . . or to distance yourself from His plan for your life.

Today, you will face many opportunities to say "yes" to your Creator—and you will also encounter many opportunities to say "no" to Him. Your answers will determine the quality of your day and the direction of your life, so answer carefully . . . very carefully.

We all go through pain and sorrow, but the presence of God, like a warm, comforting blanket, can shield us and protect us, and allow the deep inner joy to surface, even in the most devastating circumstances.
Barbara Johnson

Our heavenly Father never takes anything from his children unless he means to give them something better.
George Mueller

Figuring Out Your Faith: Write down a few of your own ideas about saying yes to God.

_____

_____

_____

_____

_____

Always Remember That Jesus Is Your Best Friend

Therefore if any man be in Christ, he is a new creature:
old things are passed away; behold,
all things are become new.

2 Corinthians 5:17 KJV

Our circumstances change but Jesus does not. Even when the world seems to be trembling between our feet, Jesus remains the spiritual bedrock that cannot be moved.

The old familiar hymn begins, "What a friend we have in Jesus . . . ." No truer words were ever penned. Jesus is the sovereign Friend and ultimate Savior of mankind. Christ showed enduring love for His believers by willingly sacrificing His own life so that we might have eternal life. Let us love Him, praise Him, and share His message of salvation with our neighbors and with the world.

Jesus was the perfect reflection of God's nature
in every situation He encountered during
His time here on earth.

Bill Hybels

Jesus: the proof of God's love.

Philip Yancey

Abide in Jesus, the sinless one—which means,
give up all of self and its life, and dwell in God's will and
rest in His strength. This is what brings the power
that does not commit sin.

Andrew Murray

Figuring Out Your Faith: Write down a few of your
own ideas about your debt to Jesus.

_____

_____

_____

_____

_____

To Strengthen Your Faith, Focus on Jesus

Then Jesus spoke to them again:
"I am the light of the world. Anyone who follows Me will
never walk in the darkness, but will have the light of life."

John 8:12 Holman CSB

I s Christ the focus of your life? Are you fired with enthusiasm for Him? Are you an energized Christian who allows God's Son to reign over every aspect of your day? Make no mistake: that's exactly what God intends for you to do.

God has given you the gift of eternal life through His Son. In response to God's priceless gift, you are instructed to focus your thoughts, your prayers, and your energies upon God and His only begotten Son. To do so, you must resist the subtle yet powerful temptation to become a "spiritual dabbler."

A person who dabbles in the Christian faith is unwilling to place God in His rightful place: above all other things. Resist that temptation; make God the cornerstone and the touchstone of your life. When you do, He will give you all the strength and wisdom you need to live victoriously for Him.

> I am truly happy with Jesus Christ.
> I couldn't live without Him. When my life gets beyond
> the ability to cope, He takes over.
> Ruth Bell Graham

> Give me the person who says, "This one thing I do, and
> not these fifty things I dabble in."
> D. L. Moody

Figuring Out Your Faith: Write down a few of your own ideas about what it means to focus on Jesus.

_____

_____

_____

_____

_____

To Strengthen Your Faith, Avoid Being Judgmental

Stop judging others, and you will not be judged.
Stop criticizing others, or it will all come back on you.
If you forgive others, you will be forgiven.

Luke 6:37 NLT

Here's something worth thinking about: If you judge other people harshly, God will judge you in the same fashion. But that's not all (thank goodness!). The Bible also promises that if you forgive others, you, too, will be forgiven. Have you developed the bad habit of behaving yourself like an amateur judge and jury, assigning blame and condemnation wherever you go? If so, it's time to grow up and obey God. When it comes to judging everything and everybody, God doesn't need your help . . . and He doesn't want it.

Christians think they are prosecuting attorneys or judges,
when, in reality, God has called all of us
to be witnesses.

Warren Wiersbe

It is time that the followers of Jesus revise their
language and learn to speak respectfully
of non-Christian peoples.

Lottie Moon

Judging draws the judgment of others.

Catherine Marshall

Figuring Out Your Faith: Write down a few of your
own ideas about the dangers of being judgmental.

_____

_____

_____

_____

_____

To Strengthen Your Faith, Be Kind to Everybody

And be kind and compassionate to one another,
forgiving one another, just as God also forgave you in Christ.
Ephesians 4:32 Holman CSB

Would you like an ironclad formula for achieving happiness, success, and satisfaction? Try this: be kind to everybody.

Kindness is a choice. Sometimes, when you feel happy or generous, you may find it easy to be kind. Other times, when you are discouraged or tired, you can scarcely summon the energy to utter a single kind word. But, God's commandment is clear: He intends that you make the conscious choice to treat others with kindness and respect, no matter your circumstances, no matter your emotions.

So today, spread a heaping helping of kindness wherever you go. When you do, you'll discover that the more kindness you give away to others, the more you'll receive in return.

When you launch an act of kindness out into
the crosswinds of life, it will blow kindness back to you.
Dennis Swanberg

When you extend hospitality to others,
you're not trying to impress people,
you're trying to reflect God to them.
Max Lucado

Do all the good you can. By all the means you can.
In all the ways you can. In all the places you can.
At all the times you can. To all the people you can.
As long as ever you can.
John Wesley

Figuring Out Your Faith: Write down a few of your
own ideas about being kind to everybody.

_____

_____

_____

_____

_____

To Strengthen Your Faith, Keep Learning Every Day

*It takes knowledge to fill a home
with rare and beautiful treasures.*

Proverbs 24:4 NCV

Knowledge is found in textbooks. Wisdom, on the other hand, is found in God's Holy Word and in the carefully-chosen words of loving parents, family members, and friends. Knowledge is an important building block in a well-lived life, and it pays rich dividends both personally and professionally. But, wisdom is even more important because it refashions not only the mind, but also the heart.

When you study God's Word and live according to His commandments, you will become wise . . . and you will be a blessing to your family and to the world.

Today is your classroom: what will you learn? Will you use today's experiences as tools for personal growth, or will you ignore the lessons that life and God are trying to teach you? Will you carefully study God's Word, and will you apply His teachings to the experiences of everyday life? The events of today have much to teach. You have much to learn. So what are you waiting for?

While chastening is always difficult,
if we look to God for the lesson we should learn,
we will see spiritual fruit.

Vonette Bright

It's the things you learn after you know it all
that really count.

Vance Havner

Figuring Out Your Faith: Write down a few of your own ideas about learning.

_____

_____

_____

_____

_____

To Strengthen Your Faith, Remember That Life Is a Gift

*For whoever finds me finds life
and receives favor from the LORD.*

Proverbs 8:35 NIV

Life can be tough sometimes, but it's also wonderful—and it's a glorious gift from God. How will you use that gift? Every day, including this one, comes gift-wrapped from God—your job is to unwrap that gift, to use it wisely, and to give thanks to the Giver.

Instead of sleepwalking through life, you must wake up and live in the precious present. Each waking moment holds the potential to celebrate, to serve, to share, or to love. Because you are a person with incalculable potential, each moment has incalculable value. Your challenge is to experience each day to the fullest as you seek to live in accordance with God's plan for your life. When you do, you'll experience His abundance and His peace.

Are you willing to treat this day (and every one hereafter) as a special gift to be savored and celebrated? You should—and if you seek to Live with a capital L, you most certainly will.

Life is a glorious opportunity.

Billy Graham

People, places, and things were never meant to give us life.
God alone is the author of a fulfilling life.

Gary Smalley and John Trent

The Christian life is motivated, not by a list of
do's and don'ts, but by the gracious outpouring of
God's love and blessing.

Anne Graham Lotz

Figuring Out Your Faith: Write down a few of your
own ideas about your wonderful life.

_____

_____

_____

_____

_____

To Strengthen Your Faith, Listen to God

The one who is from God listens to God's words.
This is why you don't listen, because you are not from God.

John 8:47 Holman CSB

Sometimes God speaks loudly and clearly. More often, He speaks in a quiet voice—and if you are wise, you will be listening carefully when He does. To do so, you must carve out quiet moments each day to study His Word and sense His direction.

Can you quiet yourself long enough to listen to your conscience? Are you attuned to the subtle guidance of your intuition? Are you willing to pray sincerely and then to wait quietly for God's response? Hopefully so. Usually God refrains from sending His messages on stone tablets or city billboards. More often, He communicates in subtler ways. If you sincerely desire to hear His voice, you must listen carefully, and you must do so in the silent corners of your quiet, willing heart.

When we come to Jesus stripped of pretensions,
with a needy spirit, ready to listen,
He meets us at the point of need.

Catherine Marshall

God is always listening.

Stormie Omartian

Listening is loving.

Zig Ziglar

In the soul-searching of our lives, we are to stay quiet
so we can hear Him say all that
He wants to say to us in our hearts.

Charles Swindoll

Figuring Out Your Faith: Write down a few of your
own ideas about listening to God.

_____

_____

_____

_____

_____

To Live the Life God Wants You to Live, Remember That Material Possessions Aren't That Important

And He told them, "Watch out and be on guard against all greed, because one's life is not in the abundance of his possessions."

Luke 12:15 Holman CSB

How important are our material possessions? Not as important as we might think. In a well-balanced life, material possessions should play a rather small role. Of course, we all need the basic necessities of life, but once we meet those needs for ourselves and for our families, the piling up of possessions often creates more problems than it solves. Our real riches are not of this world. We are never really rich until we are rich in spirit.

If you've become preoccupied with money and the things that money can buy, it's time to de-emphasize things material and re-emphasize things spiritual. When you do, you'll feel better about yourself . . . and you'll begin storing up riches that will endure forever: the spiritual kind.

A society that pursues pleasure runs the risk of raising expectations ever higher, so that true contentment always lies tantalizingly out of reach.

Philip Yancey and Paul Brand

It's sobering to contemplate how much time, effort, sacrifice, compromise, and attention we give to acquiring and increasing our supply of something that is totally insignificant in eternity.

Anne Graham Lotz

The more we stuff ourselves with material pleasures, the less we seem to appreciate life.

Barbara Johnson

Figuring Out Your Faith: Write down a few of your own ideas about materialism.

_____

_____

_____

_____

_____

Remember That Actions Speak Much Louder Than Words

For the kingdom of God is not in talk but in power.

I Corinthians 4:20 Holman CSB

The old saying is both familiar and true: actions speak louder than words. And as believers, we must beware: our actions should always give credence to the changes that Christ can make in the lives of those who walk with Him.

God calls upon each of us to act in accordance with His will and with respect for His commandments. If we are to be responsible believers, we must realize that it is never enough simply to hear the instructions of God; we must also live by them. And it is never enough to wait idly by while others do God's work here on earth; we, too, must act. Doing God's work is a responsibility that each of us must bear, and when we do, our loving Heavenly Father rewards our efforts with a bountiful harvest.

Every word we speak, every action we take, has an effect on the totality of humanity. No one can escape that privilege—or that responsibility.
Laurie Beth Jones

It is by acts and not by ideas that people live.
Harry Emerson Fosdick

Never fail to do something because you don't feel like it. Sometimes you just have to do it now, and you'll feel like it later.
Marie T. Freeman

Do noble things, do not dream them all day long.
Charles Kingsley

Figuring Out Your Faith: Write down a few of your own ideas about the consequences of your actions.

_____

_____

_____

_____

_____

To Live the Life God Wants You to Live, You Must Use Your Gifts

Do not neglect the gift that is in you.

I Timothy 4:14 Holman CSB

Face it: you've got an array of talents that need to be refined—and you'll feel better about yourself when you refine them. But nobody will force you to do the hard work of converting raw talent into prime-time talent. That's a job you must do for yourself.

Today, make a promise to yourself that you will earnestly seek to discover the talents that God has given you. Then, nourish those talents and make them grow. Finally, vow to share your gifts with the world for as long as God gives you the power to do so. When you do, you'll feel better about yourself and your abilities . . . and the world will, too.

Employ whatever God has entrusted you with,
in doing good, all possible good,
in every possible kind and degree.

John Wesley

God often reveals His direction for our lives through
the way He made us . . . with a certain personality
and unique skills.

Bill Hybels

If you want to reach your potential,
you need to add a strong work ethic to your talent.

John Maxwell

Figuring Out Your Faith: Write down a few of your
own ideas about making the most of your talents.

_____

_____

_____

_____

_____

To Figure Out Your Faith, It's Important to Confront Your Doubts

Though I sit in darkness, the Lord will be my light.
Micah 7:8 Holman CSB

Doubts come in several shapes and sizes: doubts about God, doubts about the future, and doubts about our own abilities, for starters. But when doubts creep in, as they will from time to time, we need not despair. As Sheila Walsh observed, "To wrestle with God does not mean that we have lost faith, but that we are fighting for it."

If you want to strengthen your faith, face your doubts and pray about them. And while you're at it, please remember that God never leaves you, not even for an instant. He is always with you, always willing to calm the storms of life. When you sincerely seek His presence—and when you genuinely seek to establish a deeper, more meaningful relationship Him—God is prepared to touch your heart, to calm your fear, to answer your doubts, and to restore your confidence.

Mark it down. God never turns away the honest seeker.
Go to God with your questions.
You may not find all the answers, but in finding God,
you know the One who does.

Max Lucado

Doubting may temporarily disturb,
but will not permanently destroy, your faith in Christ.

Charles Swindoll

Feelings of uselessness and hopelessness are not from God,
but from the evil one, the devil, who wants to discourage
you and thwart your effectiveness for the Lord.

Bill Bright

Figuring Out Your Faith: Write down a few of
your own ideas about what to do when you have
doubts.

_____

_____

_____

_____

When You Figure Out Your Faith, You'll Realize That God Is Here

I am not alone, because the Father is with Me.

John 16:32 Holman CSB

Do you ever wonder if God really hears your prayers? If so, you're in good company: lots of very faithful Christians have wondered the same thing. In fact, some of the biggest heroes in the Bible had their doubts—and so, perhaps, will you. But when you have your doubts, remember this: God isn't on vacation, and He hasn't moved out of town. God isn't taking a coffee break, and He isn't snoozing on the couch. He's right here, right now, listening to your thoughts and prayers, watching over your every move.

As the demands of everyday life weigh down upon you, you may be tempted to ignore God's presence or—worse yet—to rebel against His commandments. But, when you quiet yourself and acknowledge His presence, God touches your heart and restores your spirits. So why not let Him do it right now?

Get yourself into the presence of the loving Father.
Just place yourself before Him, and look up into His face;
think of His love, His wonderful, tender, pitying love.

Andrew Murray

There is a basic urge: the longing for unity.
You desire a reunion with God—with God your Father.

E. Stanley Jones

If you want to hear God's voice clearly and you are
uncertain, then remain in His presence until He changes
that uncertainty. Often, much can happen during this
waiting for the Lord. Sometimes, He changes pride into
humility, doubt into faith and peace.

Corrie ten Boom

Figuring Out Your Faith: Write down a few of your
own ideas about God's presence.

_____ _____

_____

_____

_____

_____

To Live the Life God Wants You to Live, You Must Have Faith

Whoever serves me must follow me.
Then my servant will be with me everywhere I am.
My Father will honor anyone who serves me.

John 12:26 NCV

Jesus made an extreme sacrifice for you. Are you willing to make extreme changes in your life for Him? Can you honestly say that you're passionate about your faith and that you're really following Jesus? Hopefully so. But if you're preoccupied with other things—or if you're strictly a one-day-a-week Christian—then you're in need of an extreme spiritual makeover!

Jesus doesn't want you to be a run-of-the-mill, follow-the-crowd kind of person. Jesus wants you to be a "new creation" through Him. And that's exactly what you should want for yourself, too. Nothing is more important than your wholehearted commitment to your Creator and to His only begotten Son. Your faith must never be an afterthought; it must be your ultimate priority, your ultimate possession, and your ultimate passion.

You are the recipient of Christ's love. Accept it enthusiastically and share it passionately. Jesus deserves your extreme enthusiasm; the world deserves it; and you deserve the experience of sharing it.

The essence of the Christian life is Jesus:
that in all things He might have the preeminence,
not that in some things He might have a place.

Franklin Graham

The heaviest end of the cross lies ever on His shoulders.
If He bids us carry a burden, He carries it also.

C. H. Spurgeon

Figuring Out Your Faith: Write down a few of your own ideas about the condition of your faith today.

_____

_____

_____

_____

_____

To Strengthen Your Faith, You Need the Right Kind of Fellowship

So reach out and welcome one another to God's glory.
Jesus did it; now you do it!

Romans 15:7 MSG

If you genuinely want to become the kind of person who experiences a closer relationship with God, you'll need to build closer relationships with godly people. That's why fellowship with likeminded believers should be an integral part of your life. Your association with fellow Christians should be uplifting, enlightening, encouraging, and (above all) consistent.

Are your friends the kind of people who encourage you to seek God's will and to obey God's Word? If so, you've chosen your friends wisely. And that's a good thing because when you choose friends who honor God, you'll find it easier to honor Him, too.

One of the ways God refills us after failure is through the blessing of Christian fellowship. Just experiencing the joy of simple activities shared with other children of God can have a healing effect on us.

Anne Graham Lotz

Brotherly love is still the distinguishing badge of every true Christian.

Matthew Henry

I hope you will find a few folks who walk with God to also walk with you through the seasons of your life.

John Eldredge

Figuring Out Your Faith: Write down a few of your own ideas about fellowship.

_____ _____

_____

_____

_____

_____

To Strengthen Your Faith, Avoid Distractions

Look straight ahead, and fix your eyes on what lies before you. Mark out a straight path for your feet; then stick to the path and stay safe. Don't get sidetracked; keep your feet from following evil.

Proverbs 4:25-27 NLT

All of us must live through those days when the traffic jams, the computer crashes, and the dog makes a main course out of our homework. But, when we find ourselves distracted by the minor frustrations of life, we must catch ourselves, take a deep breath, and lift our thoughts upward.

Although we may, at times, struggle mightily to rise above the distractions of everyday living, we need never struggle alone. God is here—eternal and faithful, with infinite patience and love—and, if we reach out to Him, He will restore our sense of perspective and give peace to our souls.

When Jesus is in our midst, He brings His limitless power along as well. But, Jesus must be in the middle, all eyes and hearts focused on Him.

Shirley Dobson

Paul did one thing. Most of us dabble in forty things. Are you a doer or a dabbler?

Vance Havner

As long as Jesus is one of many options, He is no option.

Max Lucado

Figuring Out Your Faith: Write down a few of your own ideas about the danger of too many distractions.

_____

_____

_____

_____

Remember That It Pays to Be Courageous

*I sought the Lord, and He answered me
and delivered me from all my fears.*

Psalm 34:4 Holman CSB

We live in a world that is, at times, a frightening place. We live in a world that is, at times, a discouraging place. We live in a world where life-changing losses can be so painful and so profound that it seems we will never recover. But, with God's help, and with the help of encouraging family members and friends, we can recover.

During the darker days of life, we are wise to remember the words of Jesus, who reassured His disciples, saying, "Take courage! It is I. Don't be afraid" (Matthew 14:27 NIV). Then, with God's comfort and His love in our hearts, we can offer encouragement to others. And by helping them face their fears, we can, in turn, tackle our own problems with courage, determination, and faith.

The Lord Jesus by His Holy Spirit is with me,
and the knowledge of His presence dispels the darkness
and allays any fears.

Bill Bright

When we meditate on God and remember the promises
He has given us in His Word, our faith grows,
and our fears dissolve.

Charles Stanley

When once we are assured that God is good,
then there can be nothing left to fear.

Hannah Whitall Smith

Figuring Out Your Faith: Write down a few of your
own ideas about moving beyond your fears.

_____

_____

_____

_____

_____

Beware:
Temptations Are Everywhere

*Put on the whole armor of God, that you may be able
to stand against the wiles of the devil.*

Ephesians 6:11 NKJV

You live a temptation-filled world. The devil is hard
at work in your neighborhood, and so are his helpers. Here in the 21st century, the bad guys are working around the clock to lead you astray. That's why you
must remain vigilant.

In a letter to believers, Peter offers a stern warning:
"Your adversary, the devil, prowls around like a roaring lion,
seeking someone to devour" (1 Peter 5:8 NASB). What
was true in New Testament times is equally true in our own.
Satan tempts his prey and then devours them (and it's up
to you—and only you—to make sure that you're not one of
the ones being devoured!).

As a believer who seeks a radical relationship with Jesus, you must beware because temptations are everywhere.
Satan is determined to win; you must be equally determined
that he does not.

Jesus faced every temptation known to humanity
so that He could identify with us.

Beth Moore

Our battles are first won or lost in the secret places of our
will in God's presence, never in full view of the world.

Oswald Chambers

Flee temptation without leaving a forwarding address.

Barbara Johnson

Temptation is not a sin. Even Jesus was tempted.
The Lord Jesus gives you the strength needed
to resist temptation.

Corrie ten Boom

Figuring Out Your Faith: Write down a few of your
own ideas about temptations.

_____

_____

_____

_____

_____

Remember to Look for Fulfillment in the Right Places

I am the Gate. Anyone who goes through me will be cared for—will freely go in and out, and find pasture. A thief is only there to steal and kill and destroy. I came so they can have real and eternal life, more and better life than they ever dreamed of. I am the Good Shepherd. The Good Shepherd puts the sheep before himself, sacrifices himself if necessary.

John 10:9-11 MSG

Everywhere we turn, or so it seems, the world promises fulfillment, contentment, and happiness. But the contentment the world offers is fleeting and incomplete. Thankfully the fulfillment God offers is all encompassing and everlasting.

Sometimes, amid the inevitable hustle and bustle of daily living, we can lose sight of the real joys of life as we wrestle with the challenges that confront us. Yet fulfillment is available to people who seek it in proper places and in proper ways.

The thoughts you think, the actions you take, the prayers you pray, and the people you serve all have a powerful influence on the fulfillment that you experience.

Aristotle observed, "Happiness depends upon ourselves." And his words still apply. If you want to find fulfillment, you'll have to find it for yourself . . . starting now and ending never.

We will never be happy until we make God the source of our fulfillment and the answer to our longings.
Stormie Omartian

If you want purpose and meaning and satisfaction and fulfillment and peace and hope and joy and abundant life that lasts forever, look to Jesus.
Anne Graham Lotz

Figuring Out Your Faith: Write down a few of your own ideas about where you can find genuine fulfillment.

_____

_____

_____

_____

To Strengthen Your Faith, Pick Friends Who Are Faithful

As iron sharpens iron, a friend sharpens a friend.
Proverbs 27:17 NLT

When you hang out with positive people, you will feel better about yourself and your world—when you hang out with negative people, you won't. So here's the question: do you want to feel better about yourself and your circumstances . . . or not? The answer you give should help you determine the friends you choose to make—and keep.

If you're really serious about being an optimistic, upbeat, hope-filled Christian, make sure that your friends feel the same way. Because if you choose to hang out with upbeat people, you'll tend to be an upbeat person, too. But if you hang out with the critics, the cynics, and the naysayers, you'll find yourself becoming a cynic, too. And life is far too short for that.

The next best thing to being wise oneself is to live
in a circle of those who are.

C. S. Lewis

For better or worse, you will eventually become more
and more like the people you associate with. So why not
associate with people who make you better, not worse?

Marie T. Freeman

Yes, the Spirit was sent to be our Counselor.
Yes, Jesus speaks to us personally.
But often he works through another human being.

John Eldredge

Figuring Out Your Faith: Write down a few of your
own ideas about friends.

_____

_____

_____

_____

_____

Beware:
Addictions Will Attack Your Faith

Be sober! Be on the alert! Your adversary the Devil is prowling around like a roaring lion, looking for anyone he can devour.

I Peter 5:8 Holman CSB

If you'd like a perfect formula for low (or no) self-respect, here it is: get addicted to something that destroys your health or your sanity. If (God forbid) you allow yourself to become addicted, you're steering straight for a boatload of negative consequences, not to mention a big bad dose of negative self-esteem.

Unless you're living on a deserted island, you know people who are full-blown addicts—probably lots of people. If you, or someone you love, is suffering from the blight of addiction, remember this: Help is available. Plenty of people have experienced addiction and lived to tell about it . . . so don't give up hope.

And if you're one of those fortunate people who hasn't started experimenting with addictive substances, congratulations! You have just spared yourself a lifetime of headaches and heartaches.

One reason I'm a teetotaler is that I got so disgusted being mistreated due to a man's drinking to excess that I never have wanted to run the risk of mistreating my own family by drinking.

Jerry Clower

A man may not be responsible for his last drink, but he certainly was for the first.

Billy Graham

The soul that journeys to God, but doesn't shake off its cares and quiet its appetites, is like someone who drags a cart uphill.

St. John of the Cross

Figuring Out Your Faith: Write down a few of your own ideas about addiction.

_____

_____

_____

_____

_____

To Live the Life God Wants You to Live, You Must Be a Servant

The greatest among you will be your servant.
Whoever exalts himself will be humbled, and whoever
humbles himself will be exalted.

Matthew 23:11-12 Holman CSB

We live in a world that glorifies power, prestige, fame, and money. But the words of Jesus teach us that the most esteemed men and women in this world are not the self-congratulatory leaders of society but are instead the humblest of servants.

Are you willing to become a humble servant for Christ? Are you willing to pitch in and make the world a better place, or are you determined to keep all your blessings to yourself. The answers to these questions will determine the quality and the direction of your day and your life.

Today, you may feel the temptation to take more than you give. You may be tempted to withhold your generosity. Or you may be tempted to build yourself up in the eyes of your friends. Resist those temptations. Instead, serve your

friends quietly and without fanfare. Find a need and fill it
. . . humbly. Lend a helping hand . . . anonymously. Share a
word of kindness . . . with quiet sincerity. As you go about
your daily activities, remember that the Savior of all humanity made Himself a servant, and we, as His followers,
must do no less.

God wants us to serve Him with a willing spirit,
one that would choose no other way.
Beth Moore

Through our service to others,
God wants to influence our world for Him.
Vonette Bright

Figuring Out Your Faith: Write down a few of your
own ideas about what it means to be a servant.

_____

_____

_____

_____

_____

To Figure Out Your Faith, Make Time for Silence

Be silent before the Lord and wait expectantly for Him.
Psalm 37:7 Holman CSB

When you have doubts, remember this: God isn't on a coffee break, and He hasn't moved out of town. God isn't taking a long vacation, and He isn't snoozing on the couch. He's right here, right now, listening to your thoughts and prayers, watching over your every move.

The Bible teaches that a wonderful way to get to know God is simply to be still and listen to Him. But sometimes, you may find it hard to slow down and listen. As the demands of everyday life weigh down upon you, you may be tempted to ignore God's presence or—worse yet—to rebel against His commandments. But, when you quiet yourself and acknowledge His presence, God touches your heart and restores your spirits. So why not let Him do it right now? If you really want to know Him better, silence is a wonderful place to start.

Growth takes place in quietness, in hidden ways,
in silence and solitude.
The process is not accessible to observation.

Eugene Peterson

Silence is as fit a garment for devotion
as any other language.

C. H. Spurgeon

If you, too, will learn to wait upon God, to get alone with
Him, and remain silent so that you can hear His voice
when He is ready to speak to you,
what a difference it will make in your life!

Kay Arthur

Figuring Out Your Faith: Write down a few of your
own ideas about the value of silence.

_____

_____

_____

_____

_____

You'll Never Figure Things Out Until You Learn to Fear God

Since we are receiving a Kingdom that cannot be destroyed,
let us be thankful and please God by worshiping him
with holy fear and awe.

Hebrews 12:28 NLT

Do you possess a healthy, fearful respect for God's power? Hopefully so. After all, the lesson from the Book of Proverbs is clear: "The fear of the Lord is the beginning of knowledge, but fools despise wisdom and instruction" (1:7 NKJV). Yet, you live in a world that often ignores the role that God plays in shaping the affairs of mankind. You live in a world where too many people consider it "unfashionable" or "unseemly" to discuss the fear of God. Don't count yourself among their number.

God maintains absolute sovereignty over His creation, and His power is beyond comprehension. As believers, we must cultivate a sincere respect for God's awesome power. The fear of the Lord is, indeed, the beginning of knowledge. So today, as you face the realities of everyday life, remember this: until you acquire a healthy, respectful fear of God's power, your education is incomplete, and so is your faith.

When true believers are awed by the greatness of God
and by the privilege of becoming His children, then they
become sincerely motivated, effective evangelists.

Bill Hybels

A healthy fear of God will do much to deter us from sin.

Charles Swindoll

The remarkable thing about fearing God is that
when you fear God, you fear nothing else,
whereas if you do not fear God, you fear everything else.

Oswald Chambers

Figuring Out Your Faith: Write down a few of your
own ideas about what it means to fear God.

_____

_____

_____

_____

_____

Remember That
Sin Equals Disaster

Jesus responded, "I assure you:
Everyone who commits sin is a slave of sin."
John 8:34 Holman CSB

Because we are creatures of free will, we may disobey God whenever we choose. But when we do so, we put ourselves and our loved ones in peril. Why? Because disobedience invites disaster. We cannot sin against God without consequences. We cannot live outside His will without injury. We cannot distance ourselves from God without hardening our hearts. We cannot yield to the ever-tempting distractions of our world and, at the same time, enjoy God's peace.

Sometimes, in a futile attempt to justify our behaviors, we make a distinction between "big" sins and "little" ones. To do so is a mistake of "big" proportions. Sins of all shapes and sizes have the power to do us great harm. And in a world where sin is big business, that's certainly a sobering thought.

Before we can be filled with the Living Water, we must be cleansed of sin. Before we can be cleansed of sin, we must be convicted. And sometimes it's painful. And shameful.

Anne Graham Lotz

We cannot out-sin God's ability to forgive us.

Beth Moore

He loved us even while we were yet sinners at war with Him!

Bill Bright

There's none so blind as those who will not see.

Matthew Henry

Figuring Out Your Faith: Write down a few of your own ideas about sin.

_____

_____

_____

_____

_____

To Live the Life God Wants You to Live, You Must Learn How to Share Your Faith

*And I say to you, anyone who acknowledges Me before men,
the Son of Man will also acknowledge him before the angels
of God; but whoever denies Me before men will be denied
before the angels of God.*

Luke 12:8-9 Holman CSB

L et's get one thing straight: those of us who are Christians should be willing to talk about the things that Christ has done for us. Our personal testimonies are vitally important, but sometimes, because of shyness or insecurities, we're afraid to share our experiences. And that's unfortunate.

We live in a world that desperately needs the healing message of Christ Jesus. Every believer, each in his or her own way, bears responsibility for sharing the Good News of our Savior. And it is important to remember that we bear testimony through both words and actions.

If you seek to be a radical follower of Christ, then it's time for you to share your testimony with others. So today,

preach the Gospel through your words and your deeds . . .
but not necessarily in that order.

To take up the cross means that you take your stand for
the Lord Jesus no matter what it costs.

Billy Graham

Usually it is those who know Him that bring Him to
others. That is why the Church, the whole body of
Christians showing Him to one another, is so important.

C. S. Lewis

Figuring Out Your Faith: Write down a few of your
own ideas about your testimony.

_____

_____

_____

_____

_____

Always Remember That God Offers Each of Us the Gift of Eternal Life

For God so loved the world that He gave His only begotten Son, that whoever believes in Him should not perish but have everlasting life.

John 3:16 NKJV

Your ability to envision the future, like your life here on earth, is limited. God's vision, however, is not burdened by any such limitations. He sees all things, He knows all things, and His plans for you extend throughout eternity.

God's plans are not limited to the events of daily life. Your Heavenly Father has bigger things in mind for you . . . much bigger things. So praise the Creator for the gift of eternal life and share the Good News with all who cross your path. And remember: if you have given your heart to the Son, you belong to the Father—today, tomorrow, and for all eternity.

God loves you and wants you to experience peace and life—abundant and eternal.

Billy Graham

If you are a believer, your judgment will not determine your eternal destiny. Christ's finished work on Calvary was applied to you the moment you accepted Christ as Savior.

Beth Moore

Those of us who know the wonderful grace of redemption look forward to an eternity with God, when all things will be made new, when all our longings will at last find ultimate and final satisfaction.

Joseph Stowell

Figuring Out Your Faith: Write down a few of your own ideas about eternal life.

_____

_____

_____

_____

_____